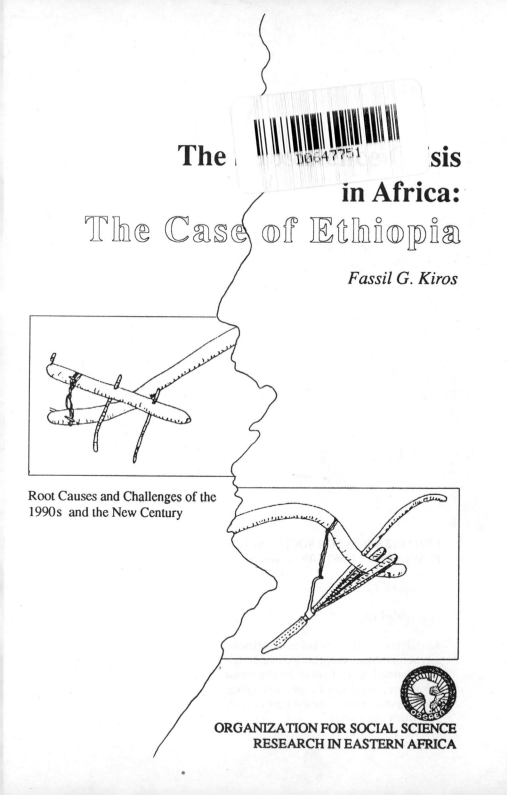

The ▮▮▮▮▮▮▮▮sis in Africa:
The Case of Ethiopia

Fassil G. Kiros

Root Causes and Challenges of the
1990s and the New Century

**ORGANIZATION FOR SOCIAL SCIENCE
RESEARCH IN EASTERN AFRICA**

**ORGANIZATION FOR SOCIAL SCIENCE
RESEARCH IN EASTERN AFRICA**

Copyright © Fassil G. Kiros

First Edition 1993

ISBN 92 9064 059 6

for Tarik

for Tarik

Acknowledgement

The author wishes to acknowledge the support and cooperation received from a number of institutions and individuals while undertaking this work.

The institutions which have provided support on different occasions are the Ford Foundation; The Rockefeller Foundation; the Institute of International Studies of the University of California at Berkeley; and jointly the Center for African Studies, Department of Economics and Institute of Food and Agricultural Sciences of the University of Florida, Gainesville.

Individuals who have generously given of their time to read and comment on earlier drafts of the manuscript are Goran Hyden, Michael J. Watts and Eshetu Chole. Bahru Zewde has also kindly commented on parts of Chapter 2 and 3.

The author extends sincere gratitude to all the institutions and individuals. However, all the findings and views expressed are those of the author and do not necessarily reflect the views of either the institutions or individuals.

Contents

List of Tables

List of Annexes

Introduction

The economic history of Ethiopia has been the history of how it has become more and more difficult for increasing numbers of rural producers to meet their minimum requirements of subsistence. It is the purpose of this book to inquire into the historical processes which have been at work, ultimately culminating in a chronic "subsistence crisis".

Considered in broad perspective, two dominant processes have been in evidence in the economic realm concerning many countries of sub-Saharan Africa especially since the 1970s. There has been on one hand an incalculable amount of financial and material resources allocated to relief and rehabilitation operations both from national and international sources. Simultaneously with this process, increasing numbers of rural people have been hurled into destitution. Indeed, the images of famine and suffering which are persistently forced upon our notice have come to symbolize the disheartening trends of our recent history.

The Ethiopian experience shows that the life-saving and rehabilitation operations have been costly. They have often overstrained existing limited national resources, facilities and management capacities. The inevitable result of this has been that less attention is given to the allocation of resources to investments ordinarily associated with long-term development. This situation, reinforced by many domestic, economic, social, political and ecological processes, and adverse international economic conditions such as the debt burden and rising reverse resource flows, have led us to a new *vicious cycle* of poverty. The new vicious cycle is not identical with that which Ragnar Nurkse popularized among students of development economics thirty years ago. It is not just a situation of "low income" and "low savings". It is a situation of falling income and spreading penury. It is not a matter of "low productivity". It is a question of declining productivity and generally the depletion of the natural resource base. It is not a question of "low-level equilibrium". It is one of an inexorable descent into the abyss of poverty.

Modest reflection will show that this scenario is a real one. It is one which is unveiled by the Ethiopian experience. We raise many difficult questions in endeavoring to understand how the process has affected most of the people of the country — the rural people. What was the nature of the national policies followed? What have been the underlying economic, social and political processes at work? What have been the effects of these policies and processes on the rural society? How can we begin to come to terms with the conditions which now prevail and to endeavor to reverse the past trends? Such are the questions we raise in this book. These are questions which may appear intimidating to many of us; and indeed they are.

The modest claim which can be made is to have raised the questions, not to have offered any final answers. It is to have raised them in what hopefully is the proper perspective. This perspective includes three main dimensions. First is the historical dimension. Second is the orientation toward a multidisciplinary approach if not such a rigorous analysis. And third is the attempt to bring into our purview factors (e.g. ecological factors) which conventionally have been regarded as *given*. It is, therefore, hoped that the justifiable criticism of students of economic development in that their approach has generally been ahistorical, narrowly disciplinary, and relatively static, can be here redressed to some degree.

While this work is based on many years of study of the problems of development in Ethiopia and on a critical examination of the available sources of pertinent information, it does not claim to be exhaustive. Indeed, a conscious attempt has been made not to overburden the reader with too much detail or to be entangled in what appear to be a seamless web of interactive processes. The temptation to take advantage of as much data as possible has in part been satisfied by including some of the available data in the annexes to the different chapters.

We begin in Chapter 1 by a glimpse of the facts and *realities* of poverty in Ethiopia today in order that the scale and depth of the problem can be better appreciated. This is followed in Chapter 2 by an explanation of the nature of the rural production system in Ethiopia and the forces which have made it increasingly difficult for the rural producers to fulfill the primordial function of "simple reproduction". Chapter 3 endeavors to highlight the direction of change which the policy of *modernization* adopted in Ethiopia since the latter part of the nineteenth century has propelled the country. This is followed by an analysis in Chapter 4 of the impact of the policy of agricultural modernization pursued during 1967–1974. Chapter 5 describes the policy of "revolutionary transformation" introduced since 1975, followed by an assessment in Chapter 6 of the impact of this policy and other related factors during this period. Chapter 7 examines the undercurrents of population growth and the degradation of agricultural land which have contributed to the deterioration of the economic conditions of the rural population and aggravated the crisis of subsistence. Chapter 8 contains the main conclusions of our inquiry which suggest a possible way out of the Ethiopian dilemma — a dilemma of poverty amidst potential plenty.

1

The Many Faces of Rural Poverty _____

INTRODUCTION

The condition which is generally regarded as a temporary "food crisis" in Ethiopia is actually the culmination of a much wider historical economic, social and political process which has evolved probably over a period of many decades. The main purpose of this introductory chapter is to examine the evidence of the many symptoms which suggest such a wider process. Before doing so, however, it would seem to be appropriate to explain the usage of the term "subsistence crisis" as applied here. This term was explained by James C. Scott in the following way:

> "The subsistence crisis level — perhaps a 'danger zone' rather than 'level' would be more accurate — is a threshold below which the qualitative deterioration in subsistence, security, status, and family cohesion is massive and painful. It is the difference between the 'normal' penury of peasant life and a literally 'hand-to-mouth' existence."[1]

This condition may manifest itself in somewhat different ways in different settings. Nevertheless, the situation in Ethiopia does suggest that such a "danger zone" may have been entered in many parts of the country by the beginning of the 1970s or earlier. We consider the evidence from which this condition might be inferred in the following pages.

THE FACTS OF RURAL POVERTY

It is well known that the countries of the third-world have been placed into different classes on the basis of poverty levels. Among the less developed are the "least developed" whose number has continued to increase during the past decade, ironically due to their own claim of this dubious distinction. For, they must plead poverty in order to obtain increasing amounts of foreign aid. What is not well known is the fact that the least developed are not all of the same level of poverty. As early as 1980 a report of the Economic Commission for Africa (ECA), for example, grouped the least developed countries of Africa into four categories on the basis of estimated per capita Gross Domestic Product (GDP). Ethiopia was then placed among the fourth of these groups, that with the lowest per capita GDP.[2]

More recent data, those of 1990, show that the estimated per capita GNP of Ethiopia was US $120 — among the lowest to be found in the category of the low-income countries of Africa and probably of other continents as well. According to this set of statistics, Ethiopia's per capita GNP in 1990 was about one-quarter that of Lesotho or Mauritania, and about one-third that of Benin, Central African Republic or Ghana (Annex 1.1).

A matter which ought to be of even greater concern is the declining trend of the per capita real product of Ethiopia since the 1960s. This situation to a very large extent reflects the dismal performance of the agricultural sector. Indeed, compared to other low-income countries, we find that the performance of the Ethiopian economy has been extremely unsatisfactory in nearly all the major sectors as well (Table 1.1). There is no denying, of course, that the periodic calamities of drought and other factors have contributed to the extremely poor performance of the Ethiopian economy. We must, however, not lose sight of the fact that what becomes something of alarm and consternation during the episode of its dramatic manifestation is that which is ordinarily unperceived — the fact that the stage which Scott refers to as the "danger zone" has been reached.

Table 1.1 Average Annual Growth Rates of Production by Major Sectors and Total GDP — 1965–1988

Group of Countries	Agriculture		Industries		Services	
	1965–80	1980–90	1965–80	1980–90	1965–80	1980–90
World Low Income	2.6	3.9	7.3	8.2	6.2	6.5
China & India	2.7	4.6	7.0	10.3	6.5	7.7
Others	2.4	2.6	8.0	3.7	5.8	4.8
ETHIOPIA	1.2	-0.1	3.5	2.9	5.2	3.7

Source: World Bank, *World Development Report 1992*, Published for the World Bank by Oxford University Press, New York, 1990, p. 220.

The economic conditions of the rural population are, of course, far worse than indicated by the averages of the national income statistics presented above. Wide gaps exist in income levels in Ethiopian society.[3] There is, therefore, little doubt that the national income figures do not reflect the income levels of most of the rural population of Ethiopia. There is, moreover, the condition of life of the nomadic pastoralists and food-gatherers whose levels of living cannot be expressed in monetary terms.

The extremely low level of income among the rural producers can be demonstrated by some data pertaining to Chilalo *Awraja* of Arsi Region. Few sub-regions in the country have received as much attention and investment as Chilalo. It was also assumed in the 1980s that agricultural producers' cooperatives (APCs) in Arsi and elsewhere would be economically better off than individual producers. It was surprising to find, however, that in 1986/87 production year, close to 50% of all the members of the cooperatives covered by a study, had earned the equivalent of less than 100 Birr (slightly over US $ 48 at the exchange rate prevailing then) per member (Annex 1.2). Considering all members of the cooperatives, the study concluded as follows:

> "When the *Awraja* average income of [cooperative members] of Birr 413.55 is divided by Arsi Region's average family size of 4.9 persons, the annual per capita income would come to Birr 84.35. [Hence], the monthly per capita income would be Birr 7.03"[4]

It was noted, however, that the authors have made no assumption that the cooperative members could survive only on the incomes received from their cooperatives. In any case, even if the average per capita income of these Chilalo agricultural producers were somewhat higher than indicated by this study, it still could not make the picture of their situation much brighter. In fact, such data do not actually inform of the many faces of rural poverty. More telling of the conditions of poverty are the facts pertaining to such indicators as food production and consumption, and the health conditions of the rural population. We therefore consider these aspects in some detail below.

THE REALITIES OF POVERTY

The Impact of Chronic Food Shortage

As a country of diverse ethnic groups and production conditions, patterns of food consumption and dietary levels are highly varied in Ethiopia. Cereals are, however, the most dominant staples in most parts of the country. *Enset* (*Ensete ventricosum*) is the main food staple for an estimated 10–15 per cent of the population. And milk is the most important source of nutrition for the pastoral nomads of the country.

For the purpose of the present discussion, we consider only the level of consumption of cereals in those regions where these are the primary sources of nutrition. Data on the other sources of nutrition are difficult to obtain. The main types of cereals produced in the country, namely maize, *teff*, barley, sorghum, wheat and millet serve as staples in various parts of the country to varying degrees. We find, however, that per capita consumption of cereals fell from about 138.4 kgs. in 1966/67 to about 94.5 kgs. in 1982/83 (Annex 1.3). However, if those regions in which *enset* is a major staple (Gamo Gofa and Sidamo) are excluded and an upward adjustment is made for increased consumption due to the production of *belg* season (so-called small-rains season), average per capita consumption would be about 150 kgs. in 1966/67 and about 113 kgs. in 1982/83, a decline of 25% during this period.

The estimated 113 kgs. annual per capita cereal consumption comes to about 60% of the per capita ration for an adult (about 500 gms. per day) which is provided to famine victims by the Ethiopian Relief and Rehabilitation Commission. The highest regional figure of per capita cereal consumption estimated for 1982/83, that of Arsi, comes to little more than the level of the famine relief ration.

The estimated average figures of cereal consumption again conceal the realities of the actual situation. It is likely that the consumption levels of a large segment of the population are less than the average estimates, as they are likely to be higher for a relatively small segment of the population. This would imply that more people are exposed to hunger than may be realized. The figures do not moreover reveal the conditions of the large number of indigents who constantly flock to the towns in search of food.

Cereals are not, of course, the only sources of calorie intake of the rural population. Still, it is found that the average calorie supply per capita in Ethiopia is not only much less than the average of all other developing countries, but has declined by about 7% during the twenty-year period between 1965 and 1986 (Table 1.2). The national estimates of calorie supply obviously conceal the relatively lower level of food consumption in the rural areas. On the whole, it is estimated that in Ethiopia, average calorie supply per capita is about 23% less than the consumption requirement.[5] As a result of this situation, malnutrition afflicts millions of Ethiopian children.[6]

Table 1.2 Daily Calorie Supply Per Capita in Ethiopia in 1965 and 1986 Compared with Levels in Other Developing Countries

Group of Countries	1965	1986
All Low-Income Countries	2046	2329
China and India	2061	2411
All others	1998	2100
ETHIOPIA	1832	1704

Source: World Bank, *World Development Report*, 1988, Published for World Bank by Oxford University Press, New York, 1988, p. 278.

Different sample studies have shown that significant proportions of children fall below the standard of weight for length as well as arm circumference. As regards the adult population, "more than 40% of the males and about 25% of the females had weights of 80% of standard or less... [and] this leanness is also confirmed by the results of measurements of arm-circumference, triceps, skinfolds, and mid-upper arm muscle circumference".[7] These conditions are largely explained by the low levels of the quantities and qualities of food consumed. The extent to which they affect the productivity of the rural producers is a matter of interest but one which would be difficult to assess.

The statistics cited above fade into insignificance when one considers the massive numbers of people who periodically succumb to the scourge of famine. The episodes of famine of the 1970s and 1980s (and indeed of the early 1990s as well) which have been of unprecedented scale and intensity are the unmistakable evidence of the "subsistence crisis".

According to Mesfin, over 25 million people were affected by famine during the period of 20 years between 1958 and 1977. This figure, according to the author was equivalent to the total rural population at least of the latter part of the period.[8] The number of deaths due to famine during this period was estimated to be between two and five million people.

The number of people affected by famine since the mid-1970s is even more alarming. According to the official estimates, close to 58 million people were affected by famine between 1973/74 and 1985/86 (Annex 1.4). This is a figure which far exceeds the estimated 1990 population of the country. The number obviously implies that millions of people have been affected by famine more than once during this period, very likely indicating an increasing rate of human casualty. In fact, the actual numbers of those killed, or of those permanently disabled will never be known. The statistics, moreover, tell none of the suffering and anguish sustained by untold numbers of Ethiopians, nor the horrifying scenes of human skeletons putting forth the last ounce of energy against the cruelty which is death by starvation.

Poverty and Ill-Health

The common form of greeting among the Amharic-speaking people of Ethiopia, — *tena yistiligne* — could well convey a message not fully appreciated. "May you be blessed with good health" is a wonderful greeting in any society. But it is so much more significant among a people always subject to the scourge or pain and suffering due to so many causes.

Nearly all of the causes of disease in Ethiopia are said to be preventable. They are attributed to such factors as malnutrition, communicable diseases, and environmental and unhygienic conditions. These are conditions which are associated with poverty. As we shall see, they are therefore *not* preventable as long as poverty prevails.

Among the common diseases resulting directly from malnutrition are described as follows:

"The prevalence of anaemia in rural populations ranges from 37.2–43.8% and successive morbidity reports confirmed that it is among the leading cause of hospitalization and hospital deaths. Another mineral deficiency is goitre which is prevalent in all regions and areas above the altitude of 2000 meters, [and] has a prevalence of 30% and particularly affects school children... Recent biochemical and clinical studies on Vitamin A in Ethiopia revealed that 16% of the children had hypovitaminosis A. ...In the general population vitamin deficiencies also occur in the form of epidemics. Outbreaks of beri-beri have occurred among migrant farm labourers, as has scurvy. In times of food shortage outbreaks of communicable disease coupled with those associated with food related toxins had devastating effects on communities. Neurolathyrism and ergotism are but recent examples".[9]

Besides the effects of malnutrition, communicable diseases account for the large majority of diseases in Ethiopia. These are obviously diseases which can be prevented by appropriate means, such as the supply of potable water, better waste disposal, personal hygiene, and immunization. The health problems caused by contaminated water supply are particularly serious. It is reported that "a relatively large proportion (over 60%) of the urban dwellers and over 90% of the rural population obtain their domestic water requirements from unreliable and contaminated sources."[10]

World statistics commonly describe the health conditions in developing countries by reporting figures pertaining to preventive and curative services made available to the population. By these statistics too few countries match Ethiopia (Table 1.3).

Such figures interest national planners and international aid providers. It is assumed that the more the number of doctors, the greater the number of children vaccinated, etc., the better the health condition of the people. This can unfortunately be misleading, for it diverts attention away from the real cause of ill health, which is poverty itself. Consider, for example, a sick child who is brought to a rural clinic for help. If fortunate, the child will receive some help. Very likely, all that the child will get is temporary relief from pain, hardly a cure. The official

Table 1.3 Some Indicators of Health Conditions in Ethiopia Compared With Those of Other Developing Countries of the World

	All Low Income Countries	China and India	Other Developing Countries	ETHIOPIA
Infant Mortality (1986)	69	56	106	155
Maternal Mortality (1980)	329*	237	607	2,000
Child Mortality (1985)	9	6	19	38
Life Expectancy (1985)	61	64	53	47
Population per Physician (1981)	6,050	2,550	17,650	88,150

*per 10,000

Source: *World Development Report*, 1988, *op. cit.*, pp. 278, 286.

statistics will then no doubt report that a child was served, that a child was saved. The chances are, however, that the child had fallen victim to illness that can be linked to malnutrition or unsanitary conditions of habitation. The likelihood of the former has been reasonably established. The latter may have to be further explained by facts which the compilers of the symptoms of poverty may find too objectionable to include in their reports.

These have to do with the condition of habitation of rural people which we describe in the following paragraphs.

The average rural household in Ethiopia consists of about five persons. And the average size of a peasant dwelling in many parts of the country consists of a single room of probably 20 square metres in area, thatched, with mud walls, and dust floor. The room would have no windows. Cooking is done on open fire in the same room often by burning dried animal dung which releases thick and less than aromatic smoke. Everyone sleeps within this single wall, literally single, for the dwelling we describe is a circular one. To many young urbanites this may sound unreal. Actually it does not even represent many households under much worse conditions of habitation. For instance, a survey undertaken a number of years ago in many rural communities has shown that the single room that we have described may be shared by at least one farm animal, such as a goat, a sheep and such other. Indeed, the number of those who were reported to be sharing their dwellings with at least one animal was strikingly significant in most areas surveyed.[11]

It is hardly necessary to dwell upon the hazards to health imposed by such conditions of habitation especially to infants and children. Nor is the situation described the worst of all possible conditions. There are after all the "homeless" and the nomadic people who are constantly exposed to many more hazards.

The foregoing descriptions of the conditions of life in Ethiopia do not tell of the numerous other ways in which poverty may manifest itself. There is for example the gender dimension of poverty which has attracted increasing attention in recent years.[12] Poverty generally weighs more heavily on female members of the rural societies. What may require even more attention is what one writer refers to as the "feminization of poverty".

"An alarming trend with potentially devastating economic, social, environmental consequences in developing Africa [is the] evidence showing that nearly two-thirds of Africa's fast growing poverty-stricken population consists of women... An estimated two-thirds of the 5 million adult refugee population on the continent are women... Even more alarming perhaps, is the fact that the feminization of poverty is becoming increasingly structural, advancing well beyond the reach of policy-makers and development projects..."[13]

The trends of economic impoverishment have, moreover, been accompanied by increasing external dependency. As in many developing countries, adverse terms of trade and balance of payments characterize Ethiopia's external economic relations. Even more serious has been the increasing dependency on food imports mostly in the form of aid donations, and the mounting burden of external financial indebtedness. It is not difficult to appreciate the implications of these trends for the future development of a country so deeply mired in abysmal poverty.

CONCLUSION

Although it is recognized that the descriptions provided above are partial, they do expose the many faces of poverty.

The plight of the rural population of Ethiopia described above is disturbing indeed. This condition has been the outcome of socio-economic and political forces which have been at work during a period of many decades. An attempt is made in the following chapters to trace the ominous trends and their root causes.

Annexes to Chapter 1

Annex 1.1 GNP Per Capita of Ethiopia and "Low-Income" Countries of Africa and the World — 1990

Countries	GNP Per Capita in US $	Ethiopia's Per Capita GNP as Percent of Others
ETHIOPIA	**120**	
Benin	360	33.3
Burkina Faso	330	36.4
Burundi	210	57.1
Central African Republic	390	30.8
Chad	190	63.2
Ghana	390	30.8
Guinea	440	27.3
Kenya	370	32.4
Lesotho	530	22.6
Madagascar	230	52.2
Malawi	200	60.0
Mali	270	44.4
Mauritania	500	24.0
Lesotho	530	22.6
Niger	310	38.7
Nigeria	290	41.4
Rwanda	310	38.7
Sierra Leone	240	50.0
Togo	410	29.3
Uganda	220	54.5
Zaire	220	54.5
Zambia	420	28.6
World Low-Income Economies	350	34.3

Source: *World Development Report, 1992.* Published for the World Bank by Oxford University Press, New York, p. 218.

Annex 1.2 Pattern of Income Distribution Among the Agricultural Producers' Cooperatives of Chilalo *Awraja* 1986/87

Wereda (Districts)	Number of APCs	Number of Members	Levels of Average Annual Income in 1986/87 (Birr)					
			Less than 100	100–300	301–500	501–900	901–1200	1200–1500
Gedeb Assasa	46	6,043	2	20	17	7	–	–
Limu & Bilbilo	43	5,078	–	19	18	6	–	–
Digelu & Tijo	25	2,444	–	9	14	1	–	–
Hitosa	24	2,201	–	1	12	10	1	1
Shirka	19	1,296	1	13	4	1	–	–
Kofelie	19	2,010	3	10	6	–	–	–
Dodota	17	1,817	–	8	4	2	2	1
Sirie	17	947	1	–	9	7	–	–
Munesa	15	874	1	6	7	1	–	–
Tyo	14	868	–	4	8	2	–	–
Ziway & Dugda	12	829	1	4	5	2	–	–
	251	24,407	9	94	104	39	3	2

Source: S. Demissie *et al.,* "The Role of Cooperatives in the Food Self-Sufficiency Program of 1986/87–1988/89", Paper presented to Food Self-Sufficiency Seminar for Representatives of District Mass and Government Organizations of Chilalo *Awraja*, Assela, Feb. 1988, p. 16 (translated by this author from the Amharic).

Annex 1.3 Rural Cereal Consumption 1966/67, 1967/68, 1979/80, 1982/83

Region	Annual Consumption Per Capita (Kgs.)			
	1966/67	1967/68	1979/80	1982/83
Arsi	180.39	230.25	130.01	190.51
Bale	125.56	n.a.	68.91	52.21
Gamo Gofa	122.64	76.54	55.10	34.24
Gojam	190.00	90.37	173.86	134.60
Gondar	183.46	101.60	179.52	176.20
Harerghe	118.99	125.06	173.56	69.32
Illubabor	103.16	136.76	159.03	120.15
Kefa	122.81	109.26	105.69	50.70
Shewa	150.13	118.30	143.57	96.16
Sidamo	119.32	33.20	11.68	30.16
Wellega	122.37	108.70	170.91	108.81
Wello	132.38	105.79	159.20	75.83
Mean Value	138.43	109.89	126.81	94.94
St. Dev.	30.07	41.47	54.63	52.94

Source: Ian Watt, "Regional and Sub-Regional Cereal Consumption Patterns, Estimates Based on a Food Balance Approach", in *Regional Planning and Development in Ethiopia* 2, P.T. Treuner, T. Kidane Mariam and T. Mulat, (Eds.), Institute of Development Research, Addis Ababa University and IREUS, University of Stuttgart, 1986, p. 223.

Annex 1.4 Estimated Population Affected by Natural and Man-Made Disasters 1973/74–1986/87 (millions)

Year	Affected by Natural Disaster	Affected by Man-made Disaster
1973/74	3.0	
1974/75	2.7	
1975/76	–	
1976/77	–	
1977/78	1.1	2.3
1978/79	4.3	
1979/80	5.2	
1980/81	3.5	
1981/82	4.4	
1982/83	5.4	1.6
1983/84	5.3	
1984/85	7.9	
1985/86	6.5	
1986/87	2.5	
	51.8	3.9

Source: Relief and Rehabilitation Commission, *Relief and Rehabilitation Commission Yesterday and Today, 1973/74–1986/87*, Addis Ababa, (June 1987), p. 10. (Report in Amharic).

References and Notes to Chapter 1

1. James C. Scott, *The Moral Economy of the Peasant*, (New Haven: Yale University Press, 1976), p. 17.
2. Economic Commission for Africa, *Quantitative Analysis of the Problems and Perspectives of the African Least Developed Countries in the Framework of the Third United Nations Development Decade*, E/CN/14/748 (Addis Ababa, 1980), p. 6.
3. Although the facts are not easy to come by, Ethiopia today does have its share of extremely rich people some of whom have made their wealth in business, often under the cover of the lucrative "subterranean" economy, not to mention those elements within the Government bureaucracy who had been among the most privileged in the society.
4. S. Demissie *et al., op. cit.*, p. 15.
5. Office of the National Committee for Central Planning, *The National Food and Nutrition Strategy for Ethiopia*, 1990, p. 21.
6. Zein Ahmed Zein, "Health and Health Services in Ethiopia, A General Survey", in *The Ecology of Health and Disease in Ethiopia*, Zein Ahmed Zein and Helmut Kloos, (Eds.), Ministry of Health, Addis Ababa, 1988.
7. Zewdie Wolde-Gebriel, "Nutrition", in *The Ecology of Health and Disease in Ethiopia, op. cit.*, p. 85.
8. Mesfin Wolde Mariam, *Rural Vulnerability to Famine in Ethiopia: 1958–1977*, (New Delhi: Vikas Publishing House Pvt. Ltd., 1984), pp. 56–67.
9. "Health and Health Services in Ethiopia, A General Survey", *op. cit.*, pp. 5–6.
10. *Ibid.*, pp. 8–9.
11. Refer to Fassil G. Kiros and Assefa Mehretu, *Survey of Socio-Economic Characteristics of Rural Ethiopia*, Institute of Development Research, Addis Ababa, 1977.

12. Refer, for example, to Lakew Woldetekle and Hirut Terefe, *Study of the Situation of Women in Ethiopia*, (Addis Ababa: Institute of Development Research), 1986; ILO, *Women's Employment Patterns, Discrimination and Promotion of Equality in Africa. The Case of Ethiopia*, Addis Ababa, 1986; *Persistent Inequalities, Women and Development*, Irene Tinker, (Ed.), (New York: Oxford University Press), 1990; *Geography and Gender in the Third World*, J. S. Momsen and J. G. Townsend, (Eds.), (Albany: State University of New York Press), 1987; UN, UNICEF, UNFPA, UNIFEM, *World's Women, Trends and Statistics, 1970–1990*, (New York), 1991.

13. Daphne Topouzis, "The Feminization of Poverty", *Africa Report*, Vol. 35, No. 3, July–August, 1990, pp. 60–61.

The Erosion of the Rural Production System _____

INTRODUCTION

The term *subsistence production* is commonly used to describe the production systems which prevail in predominantly rural societies. However, different writers tend to define the term in different ways. Among the various criteria applied to define such a system are the following: (1) the consumption of most of the production by the producers themselves; (2) the low level of hired labor and other purchased inputs used in the production process; (3) the employment of rudimentary technology in the production process; (4) the low levels of income and living standards of the producers; and (5) the slow rate of change of the system of production.[1] Several of these and other criteria are often applied to describe subsistence production. Writing in the Ethiopian context, for example, Mesfin identifies the following five characteristics of such a system:

"(i) small and often fragmented land; (ii) primitive tools and implements; (iii) production geared to personal needs rather than to market; (iv) lack of alternative seasonal employment opportunities; and (v) almost total absence of reserves of either grain or cash."[2]

The most basic features of this system of production are the fact that production is primarily aimed toward meeting household consumption needs and that the level of production which is a reflection of the rudimentary technology employed, generally affords a very low level of living. While some part of the produce may be sold by the producers, the quantities sold are usually very small. It is sometimes suggested that only producers who consume at least 50% of their produce should be regarded as subsistence producers.[3] However, studies in Ethiopia show that producers marketing as high as 50% of their produce are likely to be relatively small in number. Even in those agricultural regions which are located very close to the large urban markets, the rural producers generally offer for sale less than 20% of most types of the crops produced.[4] This is found to be the case in some other parts of Africa as well.[5]

The fact that the producers may sell a portion of their produce does not necessarily indicate that such an amount as is sold represents a *surplus* in the sense that it constitutes an amount left over after household consumption needs are fully met. Indeed, in the circumstances of most of the subsistence producers of Ethiopia, the household consumption needs are rarely met in full. This is often the case basically because of the precarious conditions of subsistence production which will be discussed below. Increasingly, however, the producers may be forced to sell a portion of their produce only to be able meet some of their cash obligations or to acquire a few of their consumption needs which they are unable to produce themselves. That the small quantities of their produce which are sold do not constitute a *surplus*, or

excess of production over consumption, is evidenced by the fact
that the producers are commonly forced to borrow grains or other
food items in order to meet their minimum consumption
requirements. Indeed, it has been argued that the produce of the
Ethiopian peasantry may last them "for only from six to nine
months" of the year.[6] It is, therefore, found that low level of living
is a condition which is typical among large segments of subsistence
producers at least in Ethiopia. As noted by the author cited at the
outset:

> "While it is true that subsistence production usually
> results in levels of living which are best described as
> abysmal poverty by most standards, it is possible,
> though rare, to find cases where the associated level
> of living is reasonably adequate."[7]

THE DIVERSITY OF RURAL PRODUCTION SYSTEMS AND INDIGENOUS TECHNOLOGIES

Scholars of peasant studies have reason to wonder whether or
not our usage of the term *subsistence production* encompasses
the *peasant mode of production*. This question must be answered,
although there is here no intention to enter the debate on the
subject of *peasantology*.[8] It should be made clear that the term
subsistence production as used here refers both to the peasant
mode of production as well as other traditional systems of
production which exist in Ethiopia as well as elsewhere in
Africa. It is well recognized that the term peasant mode of
production as used by the scholars in this field implies some
degree of participation of the producers in a wider economic
system.[9] To the extent that, as indicated above, the degree of such
participation is limited, peasant producers can be regarded as
essentially subsistence producers. Some, however, argue that the
rural producers in many parts of Africa are undergoing a process
of peasantization[10] or are straddling the twilight zone between

subsistence and commercial production.[11] As will be noted below, the Ethiopian situation may manifest some unique features in this respect.

At any rate, the peasant mode of production generally refers to the production system of only sedentary agricultural producers. As indicated above, in Ethiopia, as in other African countries, traditional production systems include other types of production as well which are neither agricultural nor sedentary. These include nomadic as well as hunting and gathering systems, which one author refers to as "survival cultures", as distinguished from "subsistence cultures" which are said to be synonymous with peasant societies.[12] The term "subsistence production" as used here encompasses all such traditional producers. In the Ethiopian situation, as we shall see, nomadic and semi-nomadic producers are not small in number. Moreover, as Mafeje has noted, the Ethiopian "peasantry" may not be all that different from the other producers at least in certain respects.

"With the development of pluralism in [Ethiopia and Sudan], large sections of the population lost their economic independence and became serving tenants or clients. However, even in such circumstances they have generally been referred to as 'peasants', which makes them indistinguishable from those producers who were in effective occupation under the communal system and the semi-nomadic pastoralists who were relatively autonomous."[13]

As already indicated at the outset, one of the main characteristics of subsistence producers has to do with the type of technology employed by such producers. It is important to appreciate the nature of the technology which has been evolved by subsistence producers. Such technology is embodied in simple implements and production processes and affords very low productivity by modern standards. It will be found that the traditional technology has often been evolved over many centuries basically in response to the demands of the natural and physical conditions of production. Each instrument or technique employed has been developed to deal with particular aspects of the production process in the most effective way possible given the range of empirical knowledge and the skills of the producers. Some scholars hold that socio-economic factors, such as population growth may act as stimuli which lead to the modification of the technology of production. According to a commonly quoted writer, Ester Boserup, population growth acts as a stimulus to technological change because of the pressure to increase production from a given stock of natural resources due to the necessity to support a larger size of population.[14]

The types of technologies evolved due to physical conditions or social stimuli would vary widely precisely because of the diversity of factors which characterize the environment. Pastoralists, for example, are generally said to employ what has been described as a "land-intensive" system whereas agriculturalists tend to employ a relatively "labor-intensive" system of production.[15] Among the agricultural producers in turn, it is possible to find the use of rudimentary technology such as the digging-stick and the hoe, or the relatively more developed technology of ox-plough agriculture which is dominant in Ethiopia.

Whatever the type of technology developed, the most basic feature is its adaptation to the natural conditions of production. Alas! This remarkable feature also turns out to be its most basic weakness. The explanations for this apparent paradox are, firstly, the fact that the natural environment to which the technology is adapted is subject to temporary and permanent changes.[16] The causes of such changes are not well understood even by the modern scientist. Secondly, the delicate balance struck with nature is also subject to disruption due to the activities of man himself often resulting from the inappropriate or excessive utilization of natural resources. Some scholars argue that integral to the traditional production system are techniques designed to ensure survival in the event of production failures. The need for survival of each production unit makes it imperative to bind itself to the wider community of subsistence producers. Such communal ties are said to be reflected in the social system described as the "moral economy"[17] or the "economy of affection"[18] which *inter alia* enable subsistence producers to survive periods of hardship.

However, rural man has all too frequently lost the struggle for subsistence. Given the instability of the natural forces, it is frequently the case for production to fall below the level required for subsistence. Subsistence production therefore implies a precarious way of life. Under such a condition, as Tawney had observed in a frequently quoted statement, the rural producer may be likened to a "man standing permanently up to the neck in water, so that even a ripple is sufficient to drown him."[19]

The precarious form of existence which characterizes one producer is also the attribute of all producers. Hence, the social system of survival insurance by a community of subsistence producers may not always suffice to enable it to survive the hardships frequently brought about by natural or social causes. Famine and consequent starvation is therefore an ever-present danger facing the producers who are thoroughly dependent on the rhythm of nature for subsistence. As potential instability is a structural feature of subsistence production, so is the threat of famine. External forces can alter the basic character for the better, or for worse as in the Ethiopian experience.

SYSTEMS OF SUBSISTENCE PRODUCTION IN ETHIOPIA

There have been few systematic and detailed studies of traditional production systems of Ethiopia. The lack of detailed knowledge about the highly diverse conditions of production continues to hamper the design of appropriate strategies of development. One of a few synoptic descriptions of Ethiopia's traditional production systems available is that provided by Westphal.[20] According to this author, four agricultural production systems can be distinguished in Ethiopia, these being "the seed-farming complex, the *enset*-planting complex, shifting cultivation, and the pastoral complex." Under the first category, the author further distinguishes five subsystems, namely the grain-plough system of the Central and Northern highlands, the barley-hoe complex connected with the pastoral production of the Oromo, the grain-plough system of Arsi and Bale Regions, the sorghum-plough system of the highlands of Harerghe, and the sorghum-hoe-terrace complex of the Konso.

Westphal's description of the seed farming system is of particular interest because of its focus on the traditional technology of production employed under various agro-ecological conditions. It is evident that the types of crop production within the various subsystems, the techniques and implements employed, the production calendar, etc. reflect the peculiarities of the basic controlling climatic and physical factors. The remarkable systems of crop rotation which have been evolved in the various regions serve as an example (Refer to Table 2.1). As Westphal has observed "any deviation from the traditional system of rotation, results in a large decrease in yield or even crop failure." Yet, after centuries of cultivation, the soils are generally still in good condition, indicating that the rotation system and customary practices have been satisfactory."[21]

The highly elaborate system of agricultural production of the Konso represents one of the best examples of how subsistence producers can effectively modify the physical environment and render it more productive. The methods of terracing, irrigation and other technological elements developed by the Konso are probably the most remarkable to be found in the country.[22]

The relationship of agricultural production systems and demographic patterns is best illustrated by the second system identified by Westphal, namely the *enset* culture. It will be found that, those parts of the country where *enset* is the main staple, are generally characterized by high population density. According to some observers, the *enset* culture is one of the most efficient systems to be found anywhere in terms of the number of people that can be supported per unit of land area. The origin, evolution and problems associated with this type of production have attracted little research so far.[23]

Table 2.1 The Complex Patterns of Crop Rotation Evolved in Parts of Arsi, Gojam and Shewa Regions

	(Second Crops Excluded)		
Year	Arsi	Gojam	Shewa
1	pea	barley	pea
2	*teff*	*teff*	wheat
3	*teff*	*teff*	*teff*
4	wheat	niger seed	linseed
5	horse bean	*teff*	lentil
6	fallow	linseed or niger seed	common bean
7	fallow	fallow	sorghum
8	fallow	fallow	barley

Source: E. Westphal, *Agricultural Systems in Ethiopia* (Wageningen: Centre for Agricultural Publishing and Documentation, 1975), pp. 96–97.

The third type of production system, shifting cultivation, is generally practised along with other forms of subsistence activities. According to a recent study, the usual combination of activities include hunting, gathering and slash-and-burn agriculture. The production system has therefore been described as the economy of "nomadic hunter-gatherers."[24] It is estimated that hunter-gatherer groups probably constitute around 200,000 people or about 8% of the total number of around 2.5 million nomadic and semi-nomadic population of the country. Among the nomadic population, the pastoralists are the dominant groups, and these control relatively large populations of the country's livestock (Annexes 2.1 and 2.2).

As indicated above, detailed studies of the traditional systems of production of Ethiopia are few and far between. These systems, which have evolved over many centuries are likely to be enormously varied and complex.[25] The foregoing synopsis is however sufficient to demonstrate the fact that the Ethiopian rural society essentially consists of highly traditional sedentary and nomadic subsistence producers. The highly diverse conditions under which they must secure their means of livelihood have made it necessary for them to evolve equally diverse methods of production which enable them to maintain a delicate balance between production and consumption. However, as will be discussed below, supply all too frequently falls below the threshold of subsistence due to the many physical problems, aggravated by social and political factors.

Physical and Biotic Problems of Production

As one observer lamented:

> "...it is Nature herself which is wicked...in spite of [man's] good faith and his courage. He sows, he works to the best of his ability, but the harvest still depends on the toss of the dice; the locusts' path, a year of drought, even an irregular distribution of rainfall and there is shortage."[26]

The problems faced by subsistence producers are many and involve climatic, pedogenic and biological conditions. The common manifestations of these are drought, excessive rain, hailstorm, flood, soil erosion, threat of wild animals, crop diseases, pests, etc. During any production season, a number of these factors could occur and cause partial or total damage to crops. Some physical environments are evidently more susceptible to certain types of production problems than others. The problems which manifest themselves within a relatively limited geographical area during a particular period can also be highly varied (Refer to Annex 2.3).

In spite of its recurrence and intensity since the early 1970s, drought is, therefore, not the only major phenomenon which causes widespread suffering to subsistence producers. It is almost certain that all of the factors identified above will strike every year in one part of the country or another causing damage of one degree or another. For example, almost at the onset of the unprecedented drought of 1983/84, extensive crop losses were being reported in many parts of the country due to *excessive rain* among other causes! More recently, in the summer of 1990, large parts of Eritrea, Tigray and Harerghe were afflicted by drought while Gambella Region suffered the catastrophic effects of flood due to excessive rain.

The nomadic or semi-nomadic populations face even more precarious conditions of production than the sedentary producers. The effects of the physical hazards are more direct and more immediate in the circumstances of the former than those of the latter. The most serious problem which causes constant anxiety particularly to nomadic pastoralists is drought. There are, however, also other problems frequently encountered by such producers, not least of which are animal diseases and the many hazards involved in the migratory form of subsistence.

Chronic food shortage is, therefore, the plight of all subsistence producers. This is not to imply, of course, that the proverbial bountiful harvests never occur, but only that they tend to be few and become even fewer due, among other things, to the secular deterioration of the physical conditions of production. The perpetual struggle for survival has, therefore, been the lot of each subsistence producer. Indeed, it is analytically significant to recognize that systems of subsistence production are essentially embedded with strategies for survival such as those referred to above. This can be appreciated from the discussions in the following paragraphs.

The Struggle for Survival

It was emphasized above that the main feature of the technology employed by subsistence producers is its adaptation to the natural and physical conditions of production. It was further stressed, however, that the conditions of production are potentially unstable. The necessity to ensure minimum subsistence has, therefore, led the traditional producers to devise ingenious methods which are integral to their production technology. These methods will vary of necessity, as they constitute responses to different conditions of production.

Among the sedentary producers of Ethiopia, the most obvious and common technique is that embodied in the practice of planting different types of crops during a particular production season. Most commonly, the cropping area is subdivided into numerous parcels each of which is planted with a particular crop.[27] Sowing of mixtures of seeds such as wheat and barley, peas and horse beans, sorghum and finger millet, etc.[28] is also practised in some parts of the country. This practice of planting different types of crops during a given season is likely to be harmonized with other techniques such as crop rotation, for example.

The number of types of crops planted by a subsistence producer during a given year can be considerable when assessed on the basis of the size of the available cropping area. Research findings show that the production of as many as five types of crops on a relatively small plot during a given year is quite common.[29] The production of so many types of crops is obviously primarily motivated by the necessity to ensure the supply of the minimum amount of food required for household consumption. The greater the number of crops planted, the greater the chance of survival of one or two types of crops in case of natural disaster. If it happens that the types of crops which survive are not the primary staples, these can still be exchanged for those which are, or for their close substitutes.

Simple observation of the practices of subsistence producers is likely to reveal any number of time-honored methods which have been evolved by such producers. This is an area of study which ought to interest agricultural scientists involved in the design of production technologies applicable in the circumstances of subsistence producers.

The production system of nomadic pastoralists is even more characteristically a system which is embedded with such methods. Among these, the most outstanding are the efforts made to increase the size of the herds and to diversify their composition. The extremely low productivity of the herd, the erratic nature of the rainfall, and the recurrence of drought compel the producers to maintain stocks over and above the immediate requirements.[30] The need also exists to form a hedge against losses due to raids, diseases, etc., conditions to which the production system is constantly exposed. The strategy of herd diversification takes account of the variation in the quality, quantity, and type of feed required to maintain different combinations of animals. Other important considerations are resistance or sensitivity to drought and disease, as well as substitutability and complementarity of the herd.[31]

The behavior of subsistence producers in response to the constant threat of natural hazards has earned them the label of "risk-averse" producers. They are often criticized for their reluctance to accept readily new techniques of production or for their lack of the venturesome quality of the modern entrepreneur. It is common knowledge, however, that few modern entrepreneurs operate under conditions in which the danger of imminent starvation is a source of constant anxiety. It is, moreover, often forgotten that such strategies as employed by nomadic pastoralists — "safety in numbers and diversification" — do have their counterparts outside the subsistence milieu as well. Consider, for example, the rush of urban dwellers everywhere to amass and stock up large amounts of products, which are not at all basic necessities, at the slightest rumor of impending shortage. Consider too the millionaire investor whose key investment strategy is the diversification of his portfolio!

Needless to say, all this is *not* to idealize the subsistence strategy of traditional producers, for our basic concern will be how to change it. To begin with, all too frequently the strategies pursued by the individual household are not necessarily always consistent with the interest of the community as a whole. Moreover, as already argued, the social insurance arrangements devised by the traditional producers based on kinship, ethnic ties, religion, etc., also turn out to be inadequate when the scale of the disaster which occurs is of such magnitude as has been frequently witnessed in the past in Ethiopia. Under these circumstances, the violence afflicted by a major catastrophe cannot be borne by those who already totter at the margin of existence. Indeed, as will be shown below the traditional system of production gradually becomes so eroded and burdened by socio-economic forces that it increasingly becomes extremely difficult to meet the very minimum subsistence requirements of the producers even under *normal* conditions.

THE IMPACT OF SOCIO-POLITICAL FORCES

In traditional Ethiopia, political power derived from the dominance and control over those who worked the land. The rise to power, and the maintenance of the hierarchy of local chiefs, warlords, and kings which ruled over the rural society for centuries were only made possible by the exploitation or outright expropriation of the rural producers. Simultaneously with this process, these producers not only bore the costs of the scramble for power, but were also themselves forced to join the many and sundry military campaigns which have characterized Ethiopian history. Given the precarious conditions of production which have already been described, the extraction of produce by the various elements could only be made at the expense of the basic necessities of the producers. As will be discussed below, the rural producers, unable to sustain the elementary function of simple reproduction, were ultimately thrown into destitution in increasing numbers.

The Burden of Tribute and Taxation

It is well known that, partly as a result of the scramble for power, numerous forms of control over the producers and of their land had evolved in Ethiopia. There is no need to go into a discussion of the maze of landholding patterns which had evolved in various parts of the country as this has been dealt with by many writers.[32] Here we limit ourselves to a brief description of the various forms and processes of exploitation of the rural producers.

During much of the early period of the country's history, the arbitrary imposition of tribute obligations was the most dominant form of exploitation. Here, we concern ourselves with the historical conditions since the early 19th century. Claims over the produce of the peasantry in particular were made in many ways and on almost any pretext. Based on his observation of the conditions which prevailed in Ethiopia in the 19th century, Plowden, for example, wrote as follows:

> "[The Chief] takes his share in kind of every grain (say a fifth), and feeds besides a certain number of soldiers at the expense of every household: he has rights to oxen, sheep, goats, butter, honey, and every other requisite of subsistence; he must be received

with joy and feasting by his subjects whenever he visits them, and can demand from them contribution on fifty pretexts — he is going on a campaign, or he has just returned from one; he has lost a horse, or married a wife; his property has been consumed by fire, or he lost his all in battle; or the sacred duty of funeral banquet cannot be fulfilled without their aid."[33]

Nor was this type of exploitation limited to the 19th century and earlier. It continued to some degree right through the first several decades of this century in many parts of the country.[34] Asbe Hailu, for example, writing in the 1920s has left a vivid description imposed by absentee landlords on the peasantry of the central highland regions of the country. Asbe's description is quoted at some length in Annex 2.4. This remarkable author describes to us in detail how the subsistence producers were rendered producers essentially for the benefit of their landlords rather than for themselves, resulting in their deprivation, suffering, and ultimately in their ignoble death and burial. The only legacy to their families, Asbe tells us, was their indebtedness of unpaid taxes and tributes.

The burden of supporting the large numbers of servants maintained by the hierarchy of rulers was also not to be underestimated. The higher the rank of the chief, the greater the number of his servants. In the words of a writer:

"The greater the household, the more refined the functions [of servants]. A man to put a master's hat on; a man to support him in the saddle; a third to hold the left side of the mule's rump in the street; and a fourth to control the right."[35]

In an equally metaphoric description, another author wrote:

"Even a [relatively] small man never goes out of doors without four retainers to accompany him. One

carries his gun, another his sword, another his purse,
and the fourth, like the man in the Chanson de
Malbrook, carries nothing at all...."[36]

Servants in the household of a local chief were, however,
relatively more fortunate members of the society when compared
with the lot of those who were reduced to begging. Indeed,
begging had become another unproductive occupation by which
large members of displaced rural producers had to maintain
themselves. Plowden had, however, exaggerated when he wrote
that "Abyssinia [was] a nation of beggars in various disguises."[37]
This occupation, it must be appreciated, was thrust upon
increasing numbers by ruthless exploitation. The society did
regard beggars with courtesy. The Amharic term commonly
used to refer to beggars, for example is *yenie bitie* meaning
literally "my type". This, however, did not imply any respect for
the occupation. On the contrary, it is intended more as an
expression of sympathy or even as a gesture to save beggars the
embarrassment of their abject condition.

Where the method of exploitation took the form of taxation,
the burden on the producers was no less onerous, if perhaps a
trifle less arbitrary. The types of taxes imposed on a single
community defied enumeration in some regions of the country.
According to one account, some 22 types of taxes could potentially be levied on the peasantry of Begemider.[38] Such taxes
varied by their purposes, forms of payments, beneficiaries, etc.
In addition to taxation in kind and in cash, the peasantry were also
expected to provide services of various sorts. Such services
could obviously be provided only at the expense of the time
required to produce their subsistence requirements. All this is not
to mention other obligations such as those, for example, imposed
by the Ethiopian Orthodox Church on its members in return for
the various religious services provided. Quite obviously, most
rural producers have had to exhaust whatever measure of energy
they still possessed by increasing the intensity of toil and

drudgery only to maintain their accustomed level of consumption. Others might have survived on borrowed food, if this could be obtained. Many had to join the services of their local chiefs as soldiers or retainers.

Even as some reforms were being introduced during the first half of this century to somewhat lessen the burden of tribute, tax and corvée labor imposed on the rural producers, the extraction of produce in the form of rent on land gained increasing predominance. As we shall see, the period of centralization of political power and modernization which began during the second half of the 19th century eventually resulted in the multiplication of the claimants of the produce of the peasantry in the form of rent. These included not only the traditional ruling classes but also the members of the new bureaucracy, the military and other elements which were able to acquire control of agricultural land through grants, purchase or expropriation. As a result, during the period preceding the 1975 agrarian reform, roughly one-half of all agricultural producers were at least partly tenants paying rent to landowners who were frequently absentee landlords (Annexes 2.5, 2.6). The payment of rent did not, however, relieve the producers from tax obligations, nor from the arbitrary demands imposed by the landowners.

The Impacts of the Scramble for Power

As soldiers or retainers, the rural producers would only increase the burden to be borne by their own kind who continued to work the land, for these latter must in one way or another provide for their maintenance as well. Indeed, soldiers were expected to loot and plunder the resources of the rural population in order to maintain themselves. The impact of war and of marauding soldiers on the rural economy, and on the rural environment had been extremely destructive throughout Ethiopia's recorded history. One observer, for example, described the Ethiopian campaigns in the following words:

"In a few days the camp would swell with warriors. The march was extraordinary. It was not merely an army moving; it was a whole population because when an Ethiopian feudal army sets out on a campaign, it was accompanied by a large number of animals and... followers that numbered three or four times the number of actual combatants. The chiefs were accompanied by their domestic servants, and not infrequently by their wives. In addition, there were wood cutters, grass cutters, supply collectors, cooks, camp organizers, and so on. Cattle, sheep, and goats were taken wherever they were found and brought along to be slaughtered in rest camps. Thus, when an Ethiopian army started to move it looked like an entire region being vacated in a hurry to escape an impending natural disaster.[39]

The effects of the movement of such a massive force can be appreciated from the following quotation by Pankhurst concerning one of King Sahle Sellassie's campaigns:

"...flourishing fields of wheat, barley and beans, the produce of toil of a rebellious tribe, were ravaged and overrun...fields and smiling meadows quickly lost their bloom under the tramp of steed...ruin and desolation were the order of the day...Far and wide the country was laid waste, and every vestige of human habitation destroyed under the torch...[The soldiers trampled] under foot the fields of ripening corn...sweeping before them the vast herds of cattle...[their] destructive progress [being] marked by the red flames that burst forth in turn from the thatched roofs of each invaded village."[40]

No claim is made here beyond providing a brief highlight of the impact of the campaigns which fill the pages of the history books. Nor is it necessary for our purposes to go into the details of these wars. We must, however, not fail to stress that the major Ethiopian campaigns were not those fought between the many warlords, but those which were directed at foreign invaders. Ethiopia's claim to the preservation of its independence is largely due to the heroic struggle and sacrifice of the rural society. In such historic campaigns as Adwa and Maichew and so many others, peasants joined the struggle in the defence of the motherland in the hundreds of thousands, often accompanied by their young sons, and carrying their own meagre provisions. Quite obviously, this meant that on one hand, the immense losses of able-bodied men and all of the other inevitable impacts of war on the other, further depleted the capacity of the rural population to maintain itself.

We must emphasize furthermore, that more recently, the rural society has also had to endure the harsh consequences of the protracted war of secession in Eritrea as well as the struggle to overthrow the Dergue regime. During the period of about a third · of a century since the early 1960s the Nation probably wasted no less resources and physical capital as a result of these wars than were devoted to development purposes. The brunt of these wars again fell on the rural population.

CONCLUSION

The forces of exploitation which brought suffering and misery to the rural society, altered the structure of the system of rural production. As the system had originally evolved, production was almost entirely for the purpose of simple reproduction. Increasingly, however, the function of production became one of supporting unproductive segments of the society born out of the scramble for dominance and conquest, and the disruption of the traditional system of production as a result of the forces described above. It must be stressed, however, that neither the diversity and complexity of the historical processes, nor their impact, have so far been adequately explored by scholars. Indeed, it would be tempting to widen the scope of this inquiry in both temporal and spatial respects. It should, for instance, be of much interest to historians to inquire into the economic and social forces which had maintained the Axumite Empire, or even those which may have flourished before it. What roles did the ancient rural producers play in the development of those civilizations and in the construction of historical symbols such as the Axumite obelisks. Similar questions can be asked about the role played by basically subsistence producers in realizing the creative and monumental accomplishments which are the rock-hewn churches of Lalibela. Would such theories as the so-called "Asiatic mode of production" have any relevance in explaining these developments? All this and much more must be left to contemporary and future historians of Ethiopia. The brief outline provided in this chapter only indicates some of the broad historical trends which are essential for a better understanding of the root causes of the subsistence crisis in our own time.

We must stress in concluding that the point is not that the rural producers ought not to have borne any of the costs of the historical processes, or of the maintenance of political order, but that they did so by the sacrifice of their very means of existence, for little was apparently done *pari passu* to alter the structures or technologies of the rural production systems.

Annexes to Chapter 2

Annex 2.1 The Nomadic Ethnic Groups of Ethiopia and their Geographic Locations

Geographic Location	Pastoral Nomads	Nomadic Hunter-Cultivators
Northern Region	Beni Amer	
Eastern Region	Afar Issa Saho Kereyou Raya Azebo	
Southeastern Region	Somali	
Southern Region	Borena Guji	
Southwestern Region	Arbore Benna Bodi Bume (Nyangatom) Geleb (Dessanech) Hammer Male Mursi Nuer Tsemai	 Tirma Chai Bale Mee'n Kwegu
Western Region		Gummuz

Source: Relief and Rehabilitation Commission (RRC) and United Nations Development Programme, (UNDP), *A Study of Nomadic Areas for Settlement* Part II. *The Socio-Economic Aspects*, Addis Ababa, Sept. 1983, p. 3.

Annex 2.2 Estimates of Ethiopia's Total and Nomadic Herds ('000)

Type of Animals	Total	Nomadic	Percent Nomadic/Total
Cattle	26350	6350	24
Sheep	21280	4890	23
Goats	15850	5170	33
Equines	6730	1350	20
Camels	1000	1000	100

Source: RRC, UNDP, *The Nomadic Areas of Ethiopia, Study Report,* Part III
   B, 1984. Computed from data summarized in Table 7, p. 29.

Annex 2.3 Major Problems that Affect Production According to About 7,000
Ethiopian Subsistence Producers in Thirteen *Weredas* (Districts) Located in
Six Regions

Regions and *Weredas*	Problems Identified (Percent of Respondents)				
	Climatic Variation	Crop Diseases	Decline of Soil Fertility	Wild Animals	Other
Arisi					
Shirka	63	16	21	16	5
Kefa					
Kersa	23	6	77	76	5
Shewa					
Adama	70	68	31	5	6
Ambo	45	20	42	27	8
Bereh	66	26	25	25	11
Grar Jarso	71	62	60	53	17
Lume	48	55	31	23	3
Mama Midir	96	53	67	43	2
Sidamo					
Awasa Tabor	33	33	14	16	23
Tigrai					
Adwa	84	63	82	16	–
Inda Mahone	60	50	39	44	19
Wello					
Dessie Zuria	76	39	47	37	6
Were Illu	64	67	45	62	5

Source: Fassil G. Kiros and Assefa Mehretu, "Survey of Socio-Economic
   Characteristics of Rural Ethiopia". *Research Bulletins 2–14,* Institute
   of Development Research (Addis Ababa, 1975/76).

Annex 2.4 Excerpts from Asbe Hailu's Descriptions of the Conditions of the Ethiopian Peasantry

"...in general the peasantry in the central highlands...surrenders a third of his produce to the *melkegna* [landed chief] or the *shalequa* [chief, literally major] annually. The peasant also renders other labour services... Besides, the peasant has to come to Addis Ababa five times a year to pay his tribute and his dues. The detail of these tributes could be described as follows: Three times in a year he surrenders 15 *quna* [a measure of grain or flour] of flour to the *melkegna*; tribute in honey; and a tenth of his produce to the state. No sooner the peasant has unloaded the tribute due to the *melkegna* than the latter 'congratulates' the peasant for having come just at the right time to be sent to the *melkegna's quelad* [large agricultural land] somewhere beyond the Awash from where the peasant is supposed to bring a load of *teff*. The toil-torn peasant supplicates, pleads and laments: 'Oh, Sire, it is harvest time in our area and if I don't do the harvesting now, before the approaching rains, Sire I will be finished, evicted, uprooted! Oh, Sire!' No heedings to his pleadings and lamentations. He must go to the *quelad* and collect the load of *teff* as the *melkegna* ordered! The peasant has no choice and he submits. Cursing, like the Biblical Eyob his birthdate — i.e. his very existence, he takes to the heels in the direction of Awash. At the *quelad* the inevitable happens. The *mislenie* [local chief, representative] engages the peasant in the renovation of the *melkegna's* house on the *quelad*. That takes a good whole week's work. Only then does the peasant reach Addis Ababa with the load of *teff*. At Addis another task, another order! Endless! The peasant ... runs out of his provision and in the hope of keeping his belly full...moves after feast places — and comes back exhausted, sick and diseased. Like a sick dog with his head resting on a heap of animal dung the peasant passes his last torturing and agonizing days below the fence of the *melkegna's* compound. When at last he dies the *melkegna's* household servants carry the body on a stick and after a few scratchy digs they bury him in a ditch...A lady living nearby asks a lady of the *melkegna's* household: 'Sister, I saw a dead body leaving your household for burial today. Who could he possibly be?' asks the lady from the neighborhood. 'Don't mind him Sister,' retorts the lady from the *melkegna's* household, 'he is not of human born, he is only a *gebar* [literally a payer of tax or tribute or belonging to a subservient class of rural producers]... But on my part I do not consider the *gebar* dead, I would rather say that he passed from death to incarnated life. No sooner the *gebar* is dead and 'buried', the *melkegna* orders the *mislenie* to send him a list of unpaid taxes and dues the dead *gebar* still owed him. Then the *mislenie* after having broken the news of the death of the *gebar* to the latter's bereft family, harasses the widow into paying the taxes and tribute her husband still owed the *melkegna* at the time of his death."

Translated from the author's writing in *Barhanena Selam* by Addis Hiwet, *op. cit.*, pp. 71–73.

Annex 2.5   Percentage of Tenants in Total Farm Population and Percentage of Total Area Cultivated by Tenants

	Wholly Rented		Partly Rented		Total	
Administrative Region	Tenancy	Area	Tenancy	Area	Tenancy	Area
Arsi	45	51	7	11	52	62
Begemeder	9	1	6	1	15	2
Gamo Gofa	43	46	4	6	47	52
Gojam	13	–	7	–	20	–
Harerghe	49	46	5	15	54	61
Illubabor	73	62	2	4	75	66
Keffa	59	67	3	4	62	71
Shewa	51	55	16	17	67	72
Sidamo	37	35	2	1	39	36
Tigrai	7	7	18	6	25	33
Wellega	54	49	5	5	59	54
Wello	16	14	16	25	32	39

Source: Ministry of Land Reform and Administration, *The Major Features of the Prevailing Land Tenure System in Ethiopia* (Addis Ababa, 1971), pp. 35 and 39; Report on Land Tenure Survey of Begemeder and Simien Province (January 1970), Tigrai Province (January 1969), and Gojam Province (January 1971).

Annex 2.6   Absentee Landowners in Pre-1975 Period

	Absentee Owners Percentage	Percentage Area of Absentee Owners
Arsi	28	27
Bale	15	12
Gamo Gofa	10	42
Hererghe	23	48
Illubabor	42	42
Keffa	18	34
Shewa	35	45
Sidamo	25	42
Wellega	29	28
Wello	26	13
Average	25.1	33.3

Source: Ministry of Land Reform and Administration, *The Major Features of the Prevailing Land Tenure System in Ethiopia,* Vol. 1, Addis Ababa, 1971, pp. 33 & 39.

References and Notes to Chapter 2

1. Clifton R. Wharton, Jr., (Ed.), *Subsistence Agriculture and Economic Development*, (Chicago: Aldine Publishing Company, 1970), pp. 15–16.
2. Mesfin Wolde Mariam, *Rural Vulnerability to Famine in Ethiopia: 1958–1977*, (New Delhi: Vikas Publishing House Pvt. Ltd., 1984), p. 23.
3. Wharton, *op. cit.*, p. 13.
4. Refer for instance to Fassil G. Kiros and Asmerom Kidane, *Socio-Economic Baseline Survey of Welmera Wereda, II. Economy*, (Addis Ababa: Ethiopian Science and Technology Commission *et al.*, 1979), p. 12.
5. Mohamed Lamine Gakou, *The Crisis in African Agriculture* (London and New Jersey: The United Nations University, 1987), p. 46.
6. Mesfin Wolde Mariam, *op. cit.*, p. 24.
7. Wharton, *op. cit.*, p. 13.
8. The reluctance to enter the debate on the subject is due to the belief that it may not be fruitful in the present discourse. As John S. Saul has stated, in the African context, the controversy on the subject "easily degenerates into a mere word-game", "African Peasants and Revolution", *Review of African Political Economy*, No. 1 (August–November, 1974, p. 45). According to Seavoy, another author, H.A. Landsberger, has concluded that the term *peasant* is so confused that it ought to be discarded. Seavoy, moreover, holds that the social value which defines the practices of peasants is the "ethic of indolence which assumes that indolence is the preferred human condition.... Peasants households are unwilling to expend any more labor than is necessary to grow enough food, produce seed for the next crop, pay a tithe to the clergy or money lender, satisfy exchange needs, and pay their taxes or rent obligations that require money".

There is, however, an apparent contradiction in these statements. Thus, it is not understandable how the various forms of extraction can be said to reflect the presence of an ethic of indolence since they obviously imply high levels of labor inputs given the rudimentary technology generally employed by peasants!, Ronald E. Seavoy, *Famine in Peasant Societies*, (New York: Greenwood Press, 1986), pp. 10–24.

The term *peasant* in any case carries with it a connotation in the minds of some people which is not at all helpful for an objective view of the peasant way of life. This may have its political origins. Well known, for example, is the reference of Marx to the peasants as a class of "barbarians," and his analogy that the isolated small holdings and backward mode of production of French peasants form a system "much as potatoes in a sack form a sack of potatoes", *The Eighteenth Brumaire of Louis Bonaparte,* (New York: International Publishers, 1935), p. 109. Indeed, there have been other characterizations of the peasantry which render Marx's comments somewhat less objectionable. Thus according to one writer, the *Declinatio Rustico* of the thirteenth century had defined "the sixth declensions of the word peasant as 'villain, rustic, devil, robber, brigand and looter, and, (in plural wretches, beggars, liars, rogues, trash and infidel)' ", Teodor Shanin, "Short Historical Outline of Peasant Societies", in *Peasants and Peasant Societies*, Teodor Shanin, (Ed.), (Oxford: Basil Blackwell, Ltd., 1987), p. 467. One wonders whether such images of peasants may still linger in the minds of some people thus affecting their perception of the predicament of peasants and of their future.

As noted in this Chapter, scholars are also not always in agreement about the possibility of analyzing the Ethiopian social structure according to conventional paradigms. In addition to the observations of Mafeje cited, refer also to

Gene Ellis, "The Feudal Paradigm as a Hindrance to Understanding Ethiopia", *The Journal of Modern African Studies*, Vol. 14, No. 2 (1976), pp. 275–295.

9. John S. Saul and Roger Woods, "African Peasantries", in *Essays on the Political Economy of Africa,* Geovanni Arrighi and John S. Saul, (Eds.), (New York and London: Monthly Review Press, 1973), p. 410.

10. K. Post, "Peasantization in Western Africa", in *African Social Studies*, P.C.W. Gutkind and P. Waterman (Eds.), (Heinemann, 1977).

11. Jossy R. Bibangambah, "Approaches to the Problem of Rural Poverty in Africa", in *Challenging Rural Poverty*, Fassil G. Kiros, (Ed.), (Organization for Social Science Research in Eastern Africa, 1985), p. 31.

12. Ronald E. Seavoy, *op. cit.*, pp. 7–8.

13. Archie Mafeje, "Peasants in Sub-Saharan Africa", *Africa Development,* CODESRIA, Vol. X, No. 3, 1985, pp. 33–34.

14. Ester Boserup, *Population and Technological Change*, (Chicago: The University of Chicago Press, 1981).

15. J. Levi and M. Havinden, *Economics of African Agriculture* 17, (Longman Group Limited, 1982), pp. 9–10.

16. This is a point discussed in Michael Watts, *Silent Violence, Food and Peasantry in Northern Nigeria*, (Berkeley, Los Angeles, London: University of California Press, 1983), pp. 14–17.

17. James C. Scott, *op. cit.*

18. Goran Hyden, *Beyond Ujamaa In Tanzania: Under-development and Uncaptured Peasantry*, (Berkeley and Los Angeles: University of California Press, 1980).

19. R.H. Tawney, *Land and Labour in China*, (Boston: Beacon Press, 1966), p. 77.

20. E. Westphal, *Agricultural Systems in Ethiopia,* (Wageningen: Centre for Agricultural Publishing and Documentation, 1975). Refer also to Amare Getahun, "Agricultural Systems

in Ethiopia", *Agricultural Systems* 3, 1978.

21. *Op. cit.*, p. 93.
22. *Op. cit.*, pp. 118–119.
23. Among the few Ethiopian researchers is the work of Taye Bezuneh; refer to "The Role of Musaceae in Ethiopian Agriculture: I. The Genus *Ensete*", *Acta Hortic.* Vol. 21 (1981), pp. 97–100.
24. United Nations Development Programme (UNDP) and Relief and Rehabilitation Commission (RRC), *The Nomadic Areas of Ethiopia, Study Report Part IV, Section 5 — Extension Programme for Hunter-Cultivators* (Addis Ababa, Sept., 1984), p. 2.
25. Refer for instance to Mesfin Wolde Mariam, "Problems of and Approaches to Regionalization in Ethiopia", in *Regional Planning and Development in Ethiopia* 1, P. Treuner, T.K. Mariam and T. Mulat, (Eds.), (Addis Ababa: Institute of Development Research and Stuttgart University, IREUS, 1985), pp. 73–74.
26. Andre Salifou, "When History Repeats Itself: The Famine of 1931 in Niger", *African Environment*, Vol. 1, No.2, (April 1975), p. 25.
27. Where landholdings are fragmented, this practice tends to be reinforced.
28. Westphal, *op. cit.*, p. 94.
29. Refer, for instance, to Fassil G. Kiros and Assefa Mehretu, "Survey of Socio-Economic Characteristics of Rural Ethiopia", *Bulletins 2–15* (Addis Ababa: Institute of Development Research, 1976–77).
30. This situation may appear to stand in contrast to the so-called "subsistence ethic" of peasants which according to Scott (*op.cit.*) denotes the desire to produce just enough to ensure survival and to meet external claims. But this may not necessarily be the case since the maintenance of what may appear to be relatively large herds only reflects the need for

insurance against the great hazards of the nomadic way of life.

31. *The Nomadic Areas of Ethiopia, Study Report, Part III B. op. cit.,* p. 49.

32. Refer, for instance to Richard Pankhurst, *State and Land in Ethiopian History,* Monograph in Ethiopian Land Tenure No.3, (Institute of Ethiopian Studies and Faculty of Law, Haile Sellassie I University, 1966); Merid Wolde Aregay, "Land Tenure and Agricultural Productivity", in *Proceedings of the Third Annual Seminar of the Department of History,* (Addis Ababa University, 1986), pp. 115–129; Bahru Zewde, "A Bibliographical Prelude to the Agrarian History of Pre-Revolution Ethiopia", in *Proceedings of the Third Annual Seminar of the Department of History,* (Addis Ababa University, 1986), pp. 12–16; Mahteme Sellasie Wolde Maskal, "The Land Systems of Ethiopia", *Ethiopia Observer,* Vol. 1, No. 9. pp. 228–289; Richard Pankhurst, "Tribute, Taxation and Government Revenues in Nineteenth and Early Twentieth Century Ethiopia", *Journal of Ethiopian Studies,* Vol. V., No. 2 (1967); Allan Hoben, *Land Tenure among the Amhara of Ethiopia: The Dynamics of Cognitive Descent,* (Chicago: University of Chicago Press, 1973); John Markakis, *Ethiopia: Anatomy of a Traditional Polity,* (Oxford: Clarendon Press, 1974); Alula Abate and Fassil G. Kiros, "Agrarian Reform, Structural Changes and Rural Development in Ethiopia", in *Agrarian Reform in Contemporary Developing Countries,* Ajit Kumar Ghose, (Ed.), (London and Canberra: Croom Helm, 1983).

33. W.C. Plowden, *Travels in Abyssinia and the Galla Country,* (England: Gregg International Publishers Ltd., 1972), pp. 137–138.

34. Mahteme Sellassie Wolde Maskal, *op.cit.* p. 283; refer also to Asnake Ali, "The Conditions of the Peasantry in Wello, 1917–1935: A Review of the Traditions", in *Proceedings of*

the Third Annual Seminar of the Department of History,
op.cit., pp. 1–7.

35. Quoted by Pankhurst, *Economic History of Ethiopia, op. cit.*, p. 38.

36. *Ibid.*

37. Plowden, *op. cit.*, pp. 404–408.

38. Mahteme Sellassie Wolde Maskal, *ibid.*

39. Teferi Teklehaimanot, "The Ethiopian Feudal Army and Its Wars, 1868–1936", Unpublished Dissertation, Kansas State University, 1971, pp. 17–18.

40. Quoted by Richard Pankhurst, *Economic History of Ethiopia, op. cit.* p. 563. Refer also to Tesfaye Teshome, "The Impact of War on the Degradation of Ecology and Environment", Paper presented to Symposium on the Problems of Peace and Development in Ethiopia, Addis Ababa, 1990.

Aspects of Modernization Policy and its Impact on the Rural Society _____

THE ORIGIN AND EVOLUTION OF MODERNIZATION IN ETHIOPIA

The people of Ethiopia take great pride in the ancient civilization of their country. Much esteemed relics of the past which remain to this day testify to the achievements which had been reached by their ancient forebears. The historical processes which had produced Ethiopia's splendid civilizations appear, however, to have been arrested long before the dawn of the era of *modernization*. The traditional society was barely touched by modernization until the early part of this century. Indeed, modernization is largely a phenomenon of the twentieth century although, as we shall see, its origins can be traced to the middle of the 19th century.

Different interpretations have been given to the concept of modernization; indeed the concept has been a subject of much theoretical controversy. Of particular interest here is a basic aspect of the concept described by one theorist in the field:

"Historically, modernization is the process of change towards those types of social, economic and political systems that have developed in Western Europe and North America from the seventeenth century to the nineteenth and have then spread to other European countries and in the nineteenth and twentieth centuries to the South American, Asian and African continents."[1]

Another author generally concurs with this description:

"In practice, modernization thus was very much the same as Westernization, i.e. the underdeveloped country should emulate those institutions that were characteristic of the rich, Western countries".[2]

This interpretation, it has been argued, represents an ethnocentric perspective. It is remarkable, however, that the early notion of modernization in the specific circumstances of Ethiopia appeared to reflect a similar perspective. This can be inferred from the meaning suggested by the Amharic term *zemenawi silitanie* which roughly means *modernity* or *modernization*. As explained elsewhere, the verb *seletene* from which *silitanie* is derived, literally means to acquire new knowledge or to be trained in new ways of doing things. Hence, based on its etymological origin, the term *silitanie* indicates the process or outcome of acquisition of new or modern ways of doing things or the adoption of modern styles of life and behavior.[3] The new model to be emulated was Western in origin; hence modernization essentially meant Westernization in the Ethiopian case as well.

It should be noted that modernization theorists often focus attention on the role played by the so-called *modernizing elites*. As explained by one of the authors cited above:

"It is these groups — political, bureaucratic, intellectual (and often military) — which are charged with the articulation of development goals and

supervision of development strategies for their
countries, and with the task of 'nation-building', i.e.,
of creating viable national societies from their socially
and culturally diverse population."[4]

Bureaucratic and intellectual groups had barely begun to
appear in Ethiopia until the early part of the twentieth century.
The scholars of Ethiopian studies tend to refer only to the
traditional pattern of social stratification which prevailed, namely
the "classic trinity of noble, priest and peasant."[5] One is hardly
justified to ascribe the functions of *modernizing elites* (as described above) to any such categories. At the same time, the role
played by the Ethiopian monarchs in initiating and promoting
modernization policy must be acknowledged. To Emperor
Menelik II (r.1889–1913) is due the full credit of this distinction,
even though, according to Ethiopian historians, modernization
was initiated in Ethiopia by Emperor Theodros (r.1855–1868).[6]
The scale and diversity of modernization reached much higher
levels during the reign of Emperor Haile Sellassie (r.1930–
1974). This period was interrupted by the Italian occupation of
Ethiopia during 1936–1941.

The early period of modernization witnessed the almost
single-handed efforts of Emperor Menelik, and Emperor Theodros
before him. Bureaucratic elements and approaches came to play
a much greater role during the rule of Emperor Haile Sellassie.

As we shall see, the overall impact of modernization cannot
be regarded as being positive as far as the conditions of the rural
population are concerned. Indeed, as will be shown in this
chapter, the economic burden on the peasantry tended to increase
along with the scale of modernization. Yet, the efforts of the
Ethiopian monarchs cannot be underestimated. These
modernizers were men of their own times and must be judged in
those terms.

There can be little doubt that the desire of attainment and
maintenance of political power on the part of the Ethiopian

monarchs was a major driving force underlying their policies of modernization. This is, however, by no means to imply that the impoverishment of the rural population was necessarily an intended result of the policy. This would be to fail to understand the objective social and political forces and processes operating during the particular epoch with which we are concerned. It would be relevant to remind ourselves of the often quoted statement of Marx that men make their own history, but that they do not do so as they please. In spite of the ultimate effects of Menelik's modernization policy, for example, the monarch was depicted as a man of extraordinary compassion especially where the conditions of the rural poor were concerned. At the same time it must be recognized that Menelik, and later Haile Sellassie, stood to benefit from modernization policy not only politically but also economically as well.

The general process of exploitation and extraction of resources was more or less similar throughout the period of modernization. Only during the post-1974 period did it take a different form. It would not, therefore, be necessary for our purposes to treat each phase of the modernization era separately.[7] Even the period of Italian occupation does not for our purposes necessitate separate treatment. The Italians were not only unable to penetrate deep into or have any lasting influence on the rural areas due to the patriotic resistance in these areas, but they also at least in the beginning and toward the end of their occupation more-or-less left the traditional rulers to continue their control in the rural areas.[8] Attempts to establish colonial farm settlements largely failed. As Bahru tells us:

> "The farmers lived under the constant threat of attack by the patriots' guerilla bands. Settlers who had come with wild anticipations of fast money ended up writing to their relatives back in Italy not to fall into the same trap. Thus, by the end of the period,

only 10% of the projected colonization scheme had been implemented. This contrasted sharply with the much higher level of activity in the field of commerce and industry — areas which, because of their urban location, were less subject to pressures of Resistance."[9]

We, therefore, examine below the major aspects of modernization policy and its main consequences during the entire period under consideration.

ASPECTS OF ETHIOPIA'S MODERNIZATION POLICY

The policy of modernization was part and parcel of the process of national state formation and centralization of political power which in the Ethiopian case was strongly influenced by the necessity to repel external aggression. Indeed, in the beginning, the Ethiopian kings were greatly attracted by the military power which advanced technology had bestowed on European nations.[10] The earliest major Ethiopian imports, for example, were fire-arms which were much needed mainly to defend the country against the European imperialist invaders themselves.

It must be acknowledged, however, that the policy of modernization pursued in Ethiopia since the latter part of the nineteenth century was also the result of what was a high regard which was ascribed to European civilization, and indeed to things European. It is notable, for example, that Marcus refers to Haile Sellassie's early visit to Europe as a "pilgrimage". Hence, *silitanie* in practice meant the importation and often unquestioning acceptance of knowhow and styles of life which had evolved outside the socio-economic milieu of the traditional society.[11] There was, to be sure, some initial resistance to Menelik's policy of modernization as well as to that of Haile Sellassie on the part of certain elements of the traditional society. In time, however,

Ethiopia as so many other developing countries, was to become dangerously addicted to the habit of absorbing imported ideas and ways of doing things.

We need hardly be reminded that technological knowhow, whether modern or traditional is the outcome of man's struggle to control his environment. Its importation, therefore, often amounts only to the transfer of the *product* of this process largely stripped of the context within which it has evolved. The Ethiopian experience of many decades demonstrates how such a process, with little conscious effort made to technological adaptation, can result in increasing external dependency, deepening rural exploitation, and perpetual underdevelopment. Indeed, the observation of one writer that "the tragedy of our times is that the LDC experienced the benefits of the scientific industrial revolution before its causes" seems to fit remarkably the Ethiopian experience.[12]

Modernization increasingly came to be manifested by the process of grafting a centralized state apparatus including ministerial and regional administration, the introduction of the first modern means of communication and transportation, the creation of a standing army, etc. These initial measures of modernization served as the main instruments of the centralization of state power as well as of mobilization of human and material resources which were required to defend the country against the ever-present threat of external aggression.

In addition to the creation of a centralized superstructure, and in order to support and enhance the new machinery, it was necessary to initiate other vital modernizing measures such as the introduction of modern education. Perhaps more than any other aspect, the introduction of modern education serves to illustrate the nature of the policy which was being pursued. The new schools, which were very few until the 1940s emphasized the learning of languages, particularly of French and English, as these were to be the media by which European knowhow was to be imbibed by the Ethiopian youths. Indeed, in the early period the fact alone of being able to speak these languages brought great rewards to the "educated." Where the education provided went beyond learning English or French, the necessary curricula, the teachers and the books had to be largely imported. Hence, for the relatively small number of youths who would join these schools, education in part entailed a process of alienation from their own society.

The maintenance and expansion of the new superstructures, which were initially extremely narrow in scope, necessitated at once domestic material and financial resources as well as supplies of goods and services which could not be had except by importation from abroad. Clearly, therefore, the promotion of a cash economy, the more extensive application of taxation in cash, and the expansion of domestic and foreign trade became the *sine qua non* for the realization of the objectives of modernization policy.

As a result, over a period of several decades since the turn of the century, a new economic structure had taken shape consisting of two more-or-less distinct sectors — the modern sector and the traditional sector. The former consisted of islands of the new economic activities and services which had emerged as a result of modernization policy and which catered principally to the needs of the privileged classes, old and new, who were centered in the capital city and regional towns. The latter consisted of the vast rural regions inhabited by the traditional subsistence producers who had little to gain, and indeed had so much to lose as a result of the advance of modernization.

THE IMPACT OF MODERNIZATION POLICY

The benefits of modernization policy accrued progressively to the ruling oligarchy, the landed classes, the members of the higher echelons of the new bureaucracy and military, and the emerging middle class of traders in the domestic and international spheres. As will be highlighted below, these benefits were obtained at the expense of no other than the rural population. The policy, moreover, steered the country toward increasing economic dependency. These outcomes are discussed in the following paragraphs focusing mainly on the trends up to the 1960s.

External Economic Dependency

It was no accident that the implementation of the policy of modernization in Ethiopia began to accelerate during the period of the scramble for Africa of the latter part of the 19th century. As one observer has noted: "The same historical forces that created the 'Gold Coast', the 'Ivory Coast' the Sudan and Kenya, were the ones which created modern Ethiopia too."[13] It is remarkable that the process of increasing dependency of the economy was discerned by an Ethiopian writer whose seminal work was first published in the early 1920s. In the words of this author:

"All those things which we ourselves used to produce in our own country are forgotten today. Foreign cloth and yarn have displaced our *buluko* and *gabi* and our fine *shema* [heavy, moderately heavy, and light cotton wrapping garments, respectively] as well as the fine yarn spun by our women, and they [the foreigners] have profited by all this. And what could be said concerning the instruments of production such as the hoe and axe! Not a single one of these which is made in Ethiopia is to be found today in the markets of Addis Ababa, Dire Dawa and Harar. In Tigre especially even the plough-share which the peasant uses is imported. All this is to say that since the Europeans came to our country, let alone to gain new technology, we have already forgotten much of the know-how which our forefathers had left to us. It is likely that we will come to forget all the rest as a consequence of the

railway which has been constructed between Addis
Ababa and Djibouti."[14]

Indeed, within a matter of a few decades Ethiopia found
herself locked into the familiar pattern of *l' economie de traite*, as
an exporter of raw materials and as an importer of foreign
manufactures. Data obtained for the closing years of the nineteenth
century illustrate this phenomenon (Refer to Annex 3.1). Indeed
the value of imports was already double the value of exports
during this period. About one-half of a century later, exports and
imports had increased greatly. Within a period of less than a
decade between 1945 and 1951, for example, values of
merchandise exports and imports more than doubled. The value
of imports exceeded that of exports during most of the period
since 1945, the deficit exceeding 28% of the export value as early
as 1948 (Annex 3.2).

Ethiopia's external economic relations continued to worsen
with the increasing volumes of international trade due to the
fluctuations of demand, supply and price conditions in the world
market. The balance of payments was, moreover, being burdened by rapidly increasing amounts of foreign loans and credits.
By 1963, total international debt was approaching US $100
million exceeding the total value of exports and re-exports for
that year.[15] The unremitting process of increasing external economic dependency continued along with the advance of
modernization in spite of the worsening economic condition
which such dependency entailed. As will be shown in Chapter 8,
Ethiopia today has become one of the most indebted countries of
all the least developed countries of the world.

Deepening Exploitation of the Rural Producers

The burden of modernization fell on the rural producers in
more ways than one. They were made to provide most of the
commodities of export. They provided tax revenues required for
the maintenance and expansion of the new state apparatus. And

only they could provide the food and other raw materials required for the support of the increasing numbers of dwellers of the new towns. And all this, as already stressed, with little or no change in the structure and technology of the traditional production system.

One of the most immediate consequences of the expanding bureaucratic machinery and of the swelling military and security forces was a rising demand for financial resources on the part of the Government. Government expenditures rose rapidly reflecting not only the costs of the new machinery but also those required for the maintenance of the traditional oligarchy. Domestic expenditures soon outstripped domestic revenues leading to increasing dependence on external sources of financing the total budgetary requirements.

The distribution of government expenditures reveals the overall policy being pursued. One of the first budgetary proclamations, that of 1945, for example, shows that around 40% of the total budget was allocated to institutions directly concerned with the maintenance of the new political structure (Annex 3.3). These included the Imperial Palace, the Prime Minister's Office, the Ministry of Pen as well as in part the Ministry of Interior. It was quite evident, moreover, that the budgets of all the agencies created were used largely to maintain the bureaucracies set up at their headquarters in Addis Ababa. Indeed, the available information indicates that salaries consumed the lion's share, probably 75% of the total national budget.

While the total budget of the Government in the 1940s and earlier might appear to be small in absolute terms, it was actually not so small when assessed on the basis of the capacity of the economy to generate revenues. The government budget necessitated the imposition of relatively high taxes on an economy which was still extremely backward.

One of the most outstanding consequences of the rising budgetary expenditures was the increasing dependence of the

Government on import and export taxes. Customs duties amounted to close to 33% of total revenues by 1956/57.[16] This is a clear reflection of the evolving economic structure already described above.

Direct taxes on the agricultural sector probably amounted to little more than 10% of total revenues by 1956/57. This amount appears to be relatively small in absolute terms. Among the explanations for this might be the fact that the taxes applied mainly to the Southern provinces, that Church land was exempted, and that many of the large land owners failed to honor their tax obligations. Still, it must be recognized that the direct taxes imposed on the agricultural sector including education tax, probably amounted to no less than 70% of the total direct taxes.[17]

The extent of the actual tax burden on the small rural producers must be assessed in relation to their general economic circumstances. First, it must be recognized that the rural producers being predominantly subsistence producers were always faced with extreme difficulty in meeting their tax obligations. This came to be more the case when they were required to pay the taxes in cash. In the latter situation, the taxes represented cash earned under conditions of highly exploitative market relations and, therefore, reflected only a part of the actual value of the produce which they brought to the market. Secondly, some of the other tax items under the category of indirect taxes (e.g. court fees and fines, salt taxes), at least partly or indirectly fell on the rural producers. Thirdly, it is also quite likely that the burden of tax on exports as well as on business income was in part at least passed on to the rural sector. Fourthly, it was a common practice of the landlords to pass on their tax obligations to their tenants. Clearly, therefore, the taxes on the agricultural as well as the other sectors of the economy largely fell on the shoulders of the rural producers.

Whatever the actual size of the tax burden which fell on the rural producers, it was unquestionably onerous. And this for a number of reasons. First, as stressed above modernization policy had done little to raise productivity in the agricultural sector. The extraction of taxes and produce from the agricultural sector was essentially a one-way process during much of the period under consideration. Agriculture received little investment in spite of the fact that it formed the pillar of the new economic structure. The consequence of increased extraction of taxes and agricultural produce was, therefore, to further aggravate the already extremely precarious condition of the rural producers.

Secondly, modernization had brought little change in the pattern of the relations of production by which the rural producers had been bound for generations. Indeed, the situation worsened with the increase in the number of absentee landlords who were based in the new centers of power — the capital city and the few other regional towns.

Thirdly, as already indicated, in time the traditional landed classes were joined by a new category of absentee-landlords, including elements of the new bureaucracy and military as well as a category of speculators who saw the benefits of controlling the main source of wealth, which was land. The new landowners sought to exploit the land at the expense of no other than the traditional rural producers.

The burden on the rural population tended to increase for yet another reason — the rising cost of modernization. In the absence of any improvement in agricultural productivity, the increasing costs of modernization policy in general, and those of the consumption goods and services required to maintain the modern sumptuous life styles of the privileged classes, could only be met by increasing the intensity of the exploitation of the rural population.

The Impact of Urbanization

It is not the primary purpose of this section to enter into a detailed analysis of the historical process of urbanization in

Ethiopia. The main purpose is to show how this phenomenon in the Ethiopian context deepened the exploitation of the rural sector and contributed to the final emergence of the crisis of subsistence.

The emergence and development of towns in Ethiopia goes at least as far back as the Axumite period and had reached a high point during the 17th century with the flourishing of Gondar. The appearance of these and other towns did not generally represent a pattern of urban development associated with a fundamental process of economic transformation, but rather reflected the rise and eventual decline of particular ruling dynasties for whom the towns served as the seats of power.[18] Urbanization as a more-or-less continuous and relatively widespread process of population agglomeration is more a phenomenon which is associated with the period of modernization, although the historical role played by this process did not appear to conform to the European pattern of development.

However, the population of Ethiopia remains to this day to be predominantly rural. According to the 1984 population census, the urban centers accounted for only slightly over 10% of the population of the country. Moreover, towns with a population size of less than 5,000 accounted for over 55% of all towns, and those with a population of 50,000 or more for less than 4%. Only one city, Addis Ababa, has a population of more than one million.[19] This pattern of distribution of the urban population has changed little even in the early 1990s. However, in spite of the very small degree of urbanization and the predominance of small towns, the impact of urbanization on the rural economy has been far-reaching.

The heavy cost of urbanization fell on the rural population in two ways: first, through the provision of food and other consumption requirements of the urban population, and secondly through the supply of the material and financial means required for the development of essential urban services.

As indicated above, urbanization in Ethiopia has not been characterized by mutually reinforcing processes of change involving the rural and urban areas. The driving economic forces which had characterized the early process of urbanization of Western Europe for example, namely technological changes and increasing productivity in agriculture and accelerated industrialization and rising employment in the urban sector, were absent in the Ethiopian situation. The new Ethiopian urban centers, it must be stressed, were principally centers of consumption rather than production. They depended for their consumption on the produce of the rural population as well as increasingly on imported manufactures. The total burden of their maintenance, however, ultimately fell on the rural producers.

The market-place served as the mechanism of the new form of extraction of produce.[20] A hierarchy of middlemen and speculators gradually established itself and made it its business to extract grain and agricultural produce from the rural sector by offering the least possible prices to the producers. The multitudes of rural producers who were compelled to sell small quantities of their produce were at a great disadvantage vis-a-vis the oligosponistic middlemen who dominated the rural markets and dictated the prices. In time too, manufactures of various sorts (e.g. synthetic clothing, head-dresses, mirrors, soap, cooking oil, kerosene, etc.) were brought to rural markets by traders which the rural producers were lured into purchasing. And as they came to be accustomed to the consumption of these manufactures, it became increasingly necessary to sell more of their own produce in order to acquire them. Hence, along with the process of urbanization increasing numbers of the rural producers came to be trapped into exchange relations and terms of trade which were heavily biased against them. The adverse terms of trade represented "unequal exchange" reflecting the underlying structural conditions. The market prices of the produce sold by the rural population did not reflect their actual costs of production, or the drudgery that went into their production. Those of manufactures, however, not only reflected the actual costs of production and the profits of the producers, but also all the costs and profits of the intermediaries. Thus, the rural producers were at a disadvantage both as sellers and as buyers.

The process of urbanization has obviously necessitated the creation and expansion of urban services of different types. In the circumstances of a country as economically underdeveloped as Ethiopia, many of these services, e.g. utilities, transportation and communication systems, schools, health centers, etc. were extremely costly not only to develop but also to operate. Again, a considerable part of the costs of providing these services directly or indirectly fell on the rural population. And as urbanization progressed and the urban services were increased and diversified, the burden of the cost borne by the rural sector increased.

It should be stressed in this relation that among the inevitable outcomes of urbanization in the Ethiopian context was the conspicuous bias of investment and essential services toward the urban areas. This has been a fundamental issue which was addressed by a number of writers.[21] The heavy bias in the pattern of distribution of basic education and health services was particularly conspicuous until very recently. A few cities such as Addis Ababa and Asmara accounted for the lion's share of all educational and health services.

The consequence of the urban-bias in the distribution of investment was a widening gap between the level of living of the urban and rural population. As shown in Chapter 1, the average per capita income of the rural population remains to be extremely low to this day. It is nowhere close to the current minimum wage of about US $20 per month which applies mainly to the urban sector. It must, however, be recognized that accurate estimates of the income and consumption gaps are difficult to make. It is also important to bear in mind that extremely wide gaps of income existed within the urban areas themselves. Indeed, the conditions of life for the large majority of urban dwellers in such cities as Addis Ababa are no different than those to be found in the shanty towns which are so characteristic of the developing world as a whole.

However, the benefits which have accrued to much of the urban population cannot be underestimated. This might be further appreciated by considering the advantages which education, for example conferred on those who have had access to it. In the 1950s and 1960s, for example, a clerk in the urban sector with a secondary-level education would earn an average income of Birr 2,400–3,600 a year. A university graduate with a bachelor's degree would earn an average income of Birr 5,400–6,000 a year. Hence, the average income of the "educated" according to this example might have been 25 to 60 times the estimated average per capita income of the rural population during the period under consideration. These figures, though rough estimates, provide a general idea of the relative magnitudes of benefits which education bestowed on increasing numbers of the urban population. The relatively large income of the "educated", it must be remembered, was obtained as a result of education provided at the expense of the rural population! Some might argue that the higher income of those with some level of education would be reflected in their relatively larger contribution to "production." This is, however, a highly questionable assertion.

Indeed, the urban bias of the Ethiopian educational system has had even more far-reaching consequences than has been ordinarily recognized. This was due not only to the inappropriateness of the objectives and contents of education in the rural areas, but also because of the way the educational system was structured. Thus, pupils who were fortunate enough to complete primary school in a rural area could only continue their education on the secondary level if they were able to attend such schools ordinarily to be found in district towns. The distances of these schools from the villages of the pupils were generally such as would prevent their attendance. The more motivated of the pupils would either take their provisions and temporarily find shelter in the towns or walked several hours a day to attend the schools.[22] And then, those relatively few who completed secondary school could join higher education institutions only if they moved to the regional capitals or to the capital city itself. The point of all this is that the slow movement out of the rural areas of the "educated" was essentially a one-way process. This is one of the main reasons why long after modern education was introduced in many rural areas, very few farmers are found even today with primary or secondary-level education. The benefits of education accrued primarily to the urban areas and to the educated themselves.[23]

CONCLUSION

The impact of modernization policy on Ethiopian rural society has been extremely severe. This policy which resulted in increasing external economic dependency, in the multiplication of the claimants on agricultural produce, and in the expansion of the urban centers of exploitation, exacerbated, as we shall see, by population growth and loss of productivity of agricultural land, not only further impoverished the rural population but also eventually led to the imminent danger of overall shortages of food supplies.

Ethiopia, it should be remembered, was long regarded as a potential "bread basket" for the neighboring countries of Africa and the Middle East. However, by 1962 the country had become a net importer of cereals and flours. And by 1964, the import values of these commodities amounted to over eight times those of the exports of such items (Table 3.1). It was, therefore, no surprise that the Government should turn its attention toward a

Table 3.1   Values of Imports and Exports of Cereals and Flour — 1962–1964 (Millions of Birr)

1 Year	2 Imports	3 Exports	4 2 + 3
1962	2.35	0.55	4.3
1963	2.05	1.07	1.9
1964	3.50	0.41	8.5

Source: Central Statistical Office, *Statistical Abstract, 1965*. Computed on the basis of data on pp. 109 and 115.

policy of agricultural modernization. It will be shown in the next chapter that this policy at best had very limited positive impact, and at worst led to basic socio-economic contradictions and to the further impoverishment of the rural society.

Annexes to Chapter 3

Annex 3.1   Estimated Exports and Imports of Ethiopia — April 1, 1887–March 31, 1898

Exports

Items	Amounts (Francs)
Coffee	3,500,000
Gold	1,400,000
Ivory	1,000,000
Hides	615,000
Civet	345,000
Wax	75,000
Total	6,935,000

Imports

Items	Amounts (Francs)
Cotton Textiles	7,228,000
Firearms and munitions	3,023,000
Glassware of various kinds (93% artificial ornamental pearls)	1,076,000
Woolen items	540,000
Food items (including alcoholic drinks)	439,000
Silk goods (including carpets)	249,000
Diverse	1,277,000
Total	13,832,000

Source: Shiferaw Bekele, "The Railway Trade and Politics — A Historical Survey, 1896–1935". *Thesis*, Department of History, Addis Ababa University, (1982), pp. 11–13.

Annex 3.2 Total Value of Imports, Exports and Re-Exports, and Visible Balance of Trade of Ethiopia — 1945–1964 (Millions of Birr)

Year	Imports	Exports and Re-Export	Visible Balance of Trade
1945	67.4	62.7	- 4.7
1946	94.9	76.2	-18.7
1947	121.2	98.7	-22.5
1948	124.0	96.6	-27.4
1949	119.1	94.0	-25.1
1950	105.5	91.3	-14.2
1951	147.4	151.9	4.5
1952	161.9	131.4	-30.5
1953	137.9	169.4	31.5
1954	160.1	160.3	.2
1955	168.0	162.2	- 5.8
1956	157.1	151.4	- 5.7
1957	178.4	192.0	13.6
1958	193.6	156.8	-36.8
1959	208.9	179.2	-29.7
1960	219.3	192.6	-26.7
1961	235.6	188.7	-46.9
1962	257.3	199.5	-57.8
1963	276.1	223.4	-52.7
1964	307.6	262.5	-45.1

Source: Central Statistical Office, *Statistical Abstract, 1965*, Addis Ababa, p. 107.

Annex 3.3   Budgeted Government Expenditure of the Year - Ending September 5, 1945

Items	Amount (Birr)
1. Civil List	
(a) Maintenance of Imperial Palace	600,000
(b) Civil List Pensions	180,000
(c) Royal Benefactions	500,000
(d) Public Banquets	25,000
(e) His Imperial Majesty's (H.I.M.) Aide de Camp's Office	15,000
(f) Mechanical Transport	175,000
(g) H.I.M.'s Chamberlain's Office	29,056
(h) H.I.M.'s Private Secretariat	70,410
(i) Chambers of Deputies and Senate	374.080
(j) Museum and National Library	58,852
(k) Distinguished Guests Reception Office	8,846
(l) Ichege's Office (Ecclesiastical Office)	16,026
TOTAL	2,053,174
2. Prime Minister's Office	
(a) Salaries	174,132
(b) Other Charges	46,551
TOTAL	220,683
3. Ministry of Communication	
(a) Salaries	156,000
(b) Other Expenses	62,334
TOTAL	218,334
4. Ministry of Public Works	
(a) Head Office	420,000
(b) Road and Bridge Maintenance	2,332,743
(c) Other Expenses	415,500
(d) Unforeseen Works	81,757
TOTAL	3,250,000

Contd.

5. Ministry of Education and Fine Arts
   (a) Salaries

Head Office	164,280
Addis Ababa Schools	274,230
Provincial Schools	645,340
TOTAL SALARIES	1,083,850
(b) Other Charges	488,590
(c) Subsidies for Private and Other Schools	100,000
	1,672,440

6. Ministry of Commerce and Industry

(a) Salaries	196,572
(b) Other Charges	37,875
	234,447

7. Ministry of the Interior
   (a) Salaries

Public Security	4,989,969
Other	3,720,446
TOTAL SALARIES	8,710,415
(b) Other Charges	2,260,032
TOTAL	10,970,447

8. Ministry of Agriculture

(a) Salaries	311,196
(b) Other Charges	368,443
TOTAL	679,639

9. Ministry of Foreign Affairs

(a) Salaries	867,124
(b) Other Charges	111,701
TOTAL	978,825

10. Ministry of Finance

(a) Salaries	2,008,479
(b) Other Charges	491,521
TOTAL	2,500,000

11. Ministry of War
    (a) Head Office   250,784
    (b) Imperial Armed Forces   7,725,550

         TOTAL   7,976,334

12. Ministry of Pen   1,003,158

13. Ministry of Justice
    (a) Salaries   1,259,304
    (b) Other Charges   111,800

         TOTAL   1,371,104

14. Ministry of Posts

    (a) Salaries   461,970
    (b) Other Charges   168,616

         TOTAL   630,586

15. Imperial Guards   1,959,722

16. Aviation Department   200,000

17. Unforseen Expenditure   2,023,650

    GRAND TOTAL   37,942,255

Source: Imperial Ethiopian Government, "A Proclamation to Authorize the
        Expenditure for the Government Services for the Year Ending the 5th
        of September 1945", *Negarit Gazeta,* No. 71 of 1945.

References and Notes to Chapter 3

1. Quoted from Eisenstadt by Henry Bernstein, "Modernization Theory and the Sociological Study of Development", *Journal of Development Studies,* Vol. 7, No. 1, (1970), p. 147.

2. Bjorne Hettne, *Development Theory and the Three Worlds,* (New York: Longman, 1990), p. 62; some theoretical discussion of the subject is also found in this book as well as in M.Mamdani, T. Mkandawere and Wamba-dia-Wamba, *Social Movements, Social Transformation and the Struggle for Democracy in Africa,* CODESRIA, Working Paper 1/88, 1988.

3. Refer to Kessatie Birhan Tessema, Amharic Dictionary (*Yeamarigna Mezgebe Kalat*), (Addis Ababa: Commercial Printing Press, 1958/59), pp. 176–177.

4. Bernstein, *op. cit.,* p. 145.

5. John Markakis, *Ethiopia, Anatomy of Traditional Polity,* (Oxford: Clarendon Press, 1974), p. 77.

6. Refer for example to Bahru Zewde, *A History of Modern Ethiopia, 1855–1974,* (Addis Ababa University Press, 1991), pp. 27–31.

7. Readers interested in the detailed history of the modernization period are referred to the following writings: S. Rubenson, *King of Kings,Theodros of Ethiopia,* (Addis Ababa) 1966; Donald Crummey "Theodros as Reformer and Modernizer", *Journal of African History,* X, 3 ,1969; Richard Pankhurst, "Theodros as an Innovator ", in *Kassa and Kassa, Paper on the Lives, Times and Images of Theodros II and Yohannes IV* (1855–1889), Taddese Beyene, R. Pankhurst and Shiferaw Bekele, (Eds.), (Addis Ababa: The Book Centre of A. A. University), June 1990, pp. 127–142; Tsehafie Taezaz Gebre-Sellassie, *History of the Era of Emperor Menelik II,* (Addis Ababa: 1967); Harold G. Marcus, *The Life and*

Times of Menelik II, Ethiopia, 1844–1913, (Oxford: Clarendon Press), 1975; Christine Sandford, *The Lion of Judah Hath Prevailed*, Biography of His Imperial Majesty Haile Sellassie I, (Westport: Greenwood Press, Publishers), 1972; Harold G. Marcus, *Haile Sellassie I The Formative Years, 1892–1936*, (Berkely: University of California Press), 1987; *Haile Sellassie I, My Life and Ethiopia's Progress*, (Addis Ababa), 1968. (Autobiography in Amharic).

8. Bahru Zewde, *Ibid.*, pp. 163, 167.
9. *Ibid.*, p. 165.
10. Richard Pankhurst, "Theodros as an Innovator", *op. cit.*, p. 140.
11. As an example, the author of a book on Emperor Menelik, narrates the circumstances leading to the introduction of electricity in Ethiopia. In his usual enthusiasm to adopt modern ways of doing things, Menelik was said to have imported electric chairs about which he had learned from visiting foreigners. He was, however, to discover only after the arrival of the modern instruments of death that electricity was required to apply them, of which the country had none. Menelik therefore was said to have taken steps to introduce electricity to Ethiopia. Although we cannot vouch to the veracity of this anecdote, it does reflect Menelik's almost unreserved acceptance of Western technological know-how. Refer to Paulos Gnogno, *Emperor Menelik*, (Addis Ababa: Bolie Printing Press, 1992), pp. 270–71 (Book in Amharic). Harold Marcus also tells us about Haile Sellassie's early fascination with Western lore and life : "His recently built modern home contained European furnishings. Its contrast with traditional dwellings could not have been more stark: the electric light, gold plate, gold-lettered menus wreathed in roses showed our host's appreciation of Europe". (Haile Sellassie I, *The Formative Years* — *op. cit.*, pp. 57–58).

12. Thomas T. Poleman, "World Food: Myth and Reality", *World Development*, Vol. 5, No. 5–7, p. 393.

13. Addis Hiwet, "Ethiopia, From Aristocracy to Revolution", *Review of African Political Economy*, Occasional Publication No. 1 (London, 1975), p.1; Refer also to Bahru Zewde, "The Fumbling Debut of British Capital in Ethiopia: A Contrastive Study of the Abyssinian Corporation and the Ethiopian Motor Transport Company Ltd.", in *Proceedings of the Seventh International Conference of Ethiopian Studies*, Sven Rubenson, (Ed.), (Berling: Arlov, Sweden, 1984), pp. 331–338.

14. Translated by this author from the Amharic work of Gebrehiwet Baykedagne, *Government and Public Administration, (Mengistina Yehizib Astedader)*, (Addis Ababa: Commercial Printing Press, Second Printing, 1941), pp. 79–80.

15. Central Statistical Office, *Statistical Abstract*, 1964, p. 131.

16. Central Statistical Office, *Statistical Abstract*, 1963, p. 90.

17. *Ibid.*

18. The author is aware of the emerging debate concerning the historical development and functions of towns in Ethiopia which may in future contribute to our knowledge in this area.

19. Central Statistical Office, *Population of Weredas, and Towns, by Sex, and Average Household Size, Based on the Preliminary Census Results* (Addis Ababa, 1985), pp. 139–164).

20. Refer, for example to Siegfried Pausewang, *Peasant, Land and Society*, (Munchen, Koln, London: Weltforum Verlag, 1983), pp. 67–75.

21. Refer for instance to Fassil G. Kiros, *et al.*, "The Urban Bias of Ethiopia's Development", in *Introduction to Rural Development,* Fassil G. Kiros, (Ed.), (Institute of Development

Research, Addis Ababa University, Addis Ababa, 1975), pp. 40–47; Eshetu Chole, "Urbanization and Its Effects on the Rural Ethiopian Economy," in *Urbanization in Ethiopia,* Marina Ottaway, (Ed.), (Addis Ababa University, Addis Ababa, 1974), pp. 186–197; Taye Mengistae, "Urban-rural Relations in Agrarian Change", in *Ethiopia, Rural Development Options*, S. Pausewang, F. Cheru, S. Brune and Eshetu Chole, (Eds.), (London: Zed Books Ltd.), 1990, pp. 30–37. For a broader discussion, refer to Michael Lipton, *Why Poor People Stay Poor, Urban Bias in World Development*, (Cambridge; Harvard University Press, 1980).

22. This has been studied and documented by this author. Refer for example to Fassil G. Kiros, "Education for Integrated Rural Development in Ethiopia: An Examination of the Problems of Transition", in *Education and Rural Development: Issues for Planning and Research*, D. Berstecher, (Ed.), (Paris: IIEP, UNESCO, 1985).

23. It is sometimes argued that remittances to rural areas mitigate the economic effects discussed. This has also been the case to some degree in Ethiopia particularly among the Guragie communities although the resource flows may not have been as significant as found elsewhere.

Toward a Policy of Agricultural Modernization 1967–1975 —

INTRODUCTION

Agricultural investment activities had begun to appear under different auspices since the early part of the period of modernization.[1] These investment activities were, however, aimed at producing agricultural commodities for export or for the emerging urban market. The major agricultural sector — the subsistence sector — was almost entirely neglected until the 1960s. It will be recalled that it was beginning in the 1960s that the country becomes a net importer of agricultural produce. As already explained this development was the ultimate consequence of the policy of modernization. Beginning in the latter part of the 1960s, therefore, government policy was directed toward the promotion of agricultural production, with particular emphasis on the production of food-grains. This chapter aims to undertake an overall review and assessment of the impact of the agricultural strategies which were designed and carried out to raise production particularly in the subsistence sector.

Two main types of agricultural strategies were pursued in the subsistence sector. The first consisted of a number of regional projects which aimed at promoting the production of food-grains in a few high-potential agricultural areas of the country. The second consisted of a *national* program of agricultural modernization which was intended to encompass gradually the food-grain producing subsistence sector as a whole.[2] These two strategies were not unrelated. Indeed, the latter approach was adopted as a result of the experience obtained in the implementation of the regional strategies.

In addition to the strategies which were focused on the subsistence sector, government policy in the 1960s was also committed to the promotion of commercial agriculture. Generous credits, as well as duty exemptions on imported agricultural machinery and fuel, were extended to private investors simultaneously with the implementation of the projects designed for the subsistence sector. Commercial agriculture, however, contributed little to total production and could only expand at the expense of traditional producers, and not just of the sedentary producers of Arsi and other regions, but also at the expense of the pastoral producers on whose traditional land it had begun to encroach.

The overall assessment of the agricultural strategies implemented betwen 1967 and 1975 shows that their impact on the whole had been extremely limited. Most rural producers had little to gain, and indeed some had much to lose as a result of these strategies of agricultural modernization. These outcomes might have been predictable, for the basic aim of government policy was not to achieve *rural transformation*, but rather to create the conditions for raising production and extracting the "surplus" with little changes in the prevailing production relations. In the following pages, the main features of the various projects are first discussed. This will then be followed by an overall assessment of the impact of the projects.

THE REGIONAL PROJECTS OF FO.OD-GRAIN PRODUCTION

Among many agricultural projects the world over which have attracted widespread attention is the Chilalo Agricultural Development Project of Ethiopia (CADU) supported by the Swedish International Development Agency (SIDA). A matter which may not have been as widely recognized is that Ethiopia had initiated a number of somewhat similar projects in different parts of the country. Among these, the relatively important ones were the Welaita Agricultural Development Unit (WADU) and the Adaa District Development Project (ADDP). There were also other such projects which were planned or at least partially implemented. These included the Tach Adyabo and Hadgiti Development Unit (TAHDU) and the Southern Regional Development Project (SORADEP). Little is known about these projects however. Mention should also be made of the Humera Agricultural Development Project which, in addition to the production of sesame mainly for the export market also promoted the production of sorghum. This project was, however, dominated by commercial producers, mainly of the "weekend-farmer" variety. The discussion of the following paragraphs is limited to CADU, WADU and ADDP which were primarily directed to the promotion of production among the subsistence food-grain producers.

The Chilalo Agricultural Development Project

CADU is commonly described as a "comprehensive agricultural development project." It was a project which was said to have been inspired by, if not necessarily fashioned after, the well-known experiments on integrated rural development of Comilla in Bangladesh. Chilalo *Awraja* or Sub-region of Arsi was selected as a project site, among other reasons, because of its relative accessibility, particularly with reference to the major urban market which was Addis Ababa itself. The project, it must be emphasized, was, however, designed on the basis of relatively broad objectives. The objectives included: (i) the achievement of economic and social development throughout the project area; (ii) the continued finding of suitable methods for bringing about agricultural development in Ethiopia when applied in an integrated manner; and (iii) the creation of possibilities for the application elsewhere in Ethiopia of the experiences gained by CADU.[3]

The objectives were pursued on the basis of a number of activities which were carried out during two phases of the project covering the periods 1967–1970 and 1970–1975. Among the main project activities were agricultural research, the dissemination of "innovations" such as "improved" seeds and fertilizer, and the provision of credit and marketing services. The activities also included the training of project personnel, the construction of feeder-roads, as well as water supply and afforestation programs.

CADU soon became a highly publicized project. Among the many activities which it had undertaken, the project was credited by some for the identification, through its research program, of high-yielding wheat varieties.[4] The research on animal husbandry was also reported to have yielded notable results especially as reflected in the increases of milk yields in the area. The project's research program on agricultural implements had not, however, been as successful as in the other areas.

An important measure of the success of CADU was taken to be the number of peasants which the project had reached within Chilalo *Awraja* and the quantities of grains which it was able to purchase, for the purpose of sale, from the peasantry. According to the official reports, by 1974–75 about 42,000 Chilalo peasants were made to participate to one degree or another in the CADU credit program which enabled them to obtain yield-increasing inputs supplied by the project. This would imply that nearly all the peasants in Chilalo *Awraja* had been reached. As a result, it was estimated that wheat production from high-yielding varieties increased to about 32,800 tons in 1974–75 as compared to the production of only 1,640 in 1967–68.[5] It was further reported that CADU was able to purchase for sale about 22,000 tons of grain and over 323,000 litres of milk by 1974–75.[6] However, as we shall see, in spite of these quantitative achievements, some assessments of CADU have tended to emphasize the negative outcome of the project. Indeed, as shown in Chapter 1, ultimately the benefits to the Chilalo producers were not as much as they were sometimes assumed to be.

Other Projects

Next to CADU, the other relatively well-known regional project was the Welaita Agricultural Development Unit. This project came into being in 1970 and was similar to CADU in a number of respects. The most notable differences were the fact that WADU placed special emphasis on population resettlement and that it was relatively less comprehensive in scope.

The location of WADU, Welaita, is a Sub-Region of Shewa Administrative Region, which is noted for the high density of its population. A resettlement activity was, therefore, introduced as an important component of the WADU project in order to ameliorate the problem of high population density. In addition to the resettlement program, the other main components of WADU included the development and diffusion of yield-increasing inputs, provision of credit to the peasants and the marketing of agricultural produce.[7]

In the area of the main activity of WADU during 1970–1974, less than 750 new households were resettled (in addition to the reorganization of settlement plots for some 700 households which were already settled). The actual plan was to resettle 1,050 new households during this period.

WADU also largely depended on CADU and other research centers for inputs such as improved seeds. It is estimated that over 6,000 peasants were reached by 1975 with the package of WADU's yield-increasing inputs. Yields of the main crops in the area, such as maize, wheat and *teff* were reported to have risen as a result of the application of the new package of inputs. Through its marketing services WADU was able to facilitate the sale of some of the additional produce of the peasantry.[8]

The Adaa District Development Project was initiated in 1972–73. It should be recognized that Adaa is an area well-known for the production of *teff*, which is an extremely important staple in Ethiopia, particularly in the urban centers. The District is located in the range of 50 to 60 kilometres south-east of Addis Ababa, a city so heavily dependent on the consumption of *teff*. Although other factors have no doubt been taken into account in the selection of this area for government investment, the proximity of the District to the major urban market was certainly a key consideration.[9]

The main components of ADDP included the development and diffusion of a package of yield-increasing inputs, and the provision of credit as well as marketing services to the peasants in the area. The achievements of ADDP in all these areas have not been well documented. However, as we shall see below, the overall impact of the project was probably very limited.

THE NATIONAL SCHEME OF AGRICULTURAL MODERNIZATION

As stated above, an overall assessment of the impact of the regional agricultural projects will be provided below. It is, however, pertinent to note here that the most important lesson which was learned from the implementation of the regional projects was learned quite early from the experience of CADU. It was concluded that CADU was too costly a project and hence beyond any possibility of being replicated economically in other regions. It was, therefore, decided that what was needed in the circumstances of Ethiopia was not more comprehensive projects such as CADU, but rather minimum-package programs (MPP) which could be applied to peasant agriculture throughout the country. Thus, this latter strategy was initiated in 1971. Two phases of MPP were implemented, the first covering the period 1971–1974, and the second the period 1980–85, having been delayed mainly due to the revolutionary changes taking place in the country. The discussion in this chapter is confined to the first phase; the second phase will be considered in the next chapter.

The MPP, in principle, was supposed to share some of the basic objectives of the comprehensive projects. However, in practice its activities were centered on the dissemination of a "few proven innovations" developed by adaptive research in the comprehensive project areas or at research centers. The main components of the MPP package were fertilizer and "improved" seeds. The diffusion strategy involved three different steps. In the first step, an agricultural area was selected as a zone of "observation." Information relating to the types of crops produced, soil types, number of peasant households, etc. was then compiled on the area, this to be followed by seed and fertilizer trials. Based on the findings on the "observation" stage, a decision might be reached to create a "demonstration" area. In this second stage, the main activity would be the demonstration of the package of innovations by application on the plots of "model farmers". The "MPP area" would come into being in the third stage which could take a period of three to four years after the determination of a zone of "observation." The MPP area would then be divided into five extension stations, each of which to be assigned an extension agent.

The MPP was implemented vigorously during its first phase, placed under a relatively autonomous agency of the Ministry of Agriculture — the Extension and Project Implementation Department (EPID). It was reported that by 1973–74, nearly 50,000 peasant households had been reached, and over 67,000 quintals of fertilizer and 1,200 quintals of improved seeds were distributed.[10] The number of participants and the quantities of the inputs distributed increased significantly following this period although the program was not being implemented as originally designed.

It should be noted that the MPP did not replace the existing regional projects. These latter continued to operate in their respective regions while the MPP functioned in some of the areas not covered by them. However, as we shall see, the activities of both the regional projects and the national scheme of agricultural modernization were significantly altered in the aftermath of the revolution.

AN ASSESSMENT OF THE IMPACT OF THE POLICY OF AGRICULTURAL MODERNIZATION

The Ethiopian comprehensive and minimum package projects which were implemented with much vigor between 1967 and 1974 turned out to be controversial projects. The controversy about CADU in particular began to rage even as its first phase was being implemented. However, few of the assessments of these projects which have been made were concerned about their overall impact. Many of the evaluations have generally tended to pay much attention to micro-economic considerations, or to technical matters of project organization, coordination, implementation and the like. Such analyses, which were in the nature of project evaluation, would of course serve useful purposes for the better design and implementation of more-or-less the same types of activities.[11] Their contributions to the quest for alternative and more effective approaches to rural development were, however, limited.

There have been, to be sure, some critical analyses,particularly of CADU which have brought to light the economic and political contradictions which have resulted from the implementation of the project.[12] The central question raised by such analyses had to do with the matter of who stood to benefit from the projects and particularly from the "green revolution" technology which they introduced. Of course, the question regarding the impact of "green revolution" technology was not new. Although there have been divergent perspectives regarding this subject,[13] most observers will probably be in agreement with the following general assessment of the impact of this technology:

"Where the technology has been introduced in areas characterized by a reasonable degree of equity in the distribution of resources, the effect has been favorable both in terms of productivity and equity. When the technology has been introduced in areas characterized by great irregularity in the distribution of resources, the productivity impact has been weak and the pattern of irregularity has been reinforced".[14]

With regard to CADU, Cohen observed as follows:

"A case study of this project illustrates how the new small-farm strategies emerging from the increasingly dominant rural-development model can have disastrous effects on targeted beneficiaries in areas marked by un-regulated freehold tenure... Specifically, while the project was designed to improve and develop the agrarian production of tenants and small-scale landowners, the effects of better agricultural techniques and use of improved seeds and fertilizers were communicated to surrounding landowners. Major as well as middle-sized land-owners came to realize that agriculture could be very lucrative".[15]

It was clear, therefore, that the CADU activities in reality came to serve interests which were not necessarily in consonance with those of the underprivileged rural producers. More-or-less similar comments could be made with regard to WADU, ADDP, and MPP as well. These observations must not be taken to imply as a denial that none of the subsistence producers who were exposed to the project activities have benefited from them. Some have benefited from the projects, but many too had lost their very means of livelihood as a result especially of the CADU activities, mainly resulting from the replacement of man by machine. If the project had continued to be implemented as originally designed, many more of the Chilalo tenant farmers might have been evicted as more and more landlords would turn into "capitalists". This indeed was what gave much impetus to the cry "land to the tiller" which had already begun to resound among university students in the 1960s. It was also the reason why the Swedish Government insisted on the implementation of land reform as a condition for the continued financial support of the project. Agrarian reform was to become the main outcome of the revolutionary changes which engulfed the country since 1974.

The popular debate provoked by the Ethiopian projects has, therefore, had far-reaching implications. The intention here is not to dwell upon the familiar criticisms and controversies concerning CADU and the other projects discussed above. We seek rather to raise other basic issues which concern the impact of the policy of agricultural modernization in the overall national perspective, the relevance and sustainability of the projects which were introduced, and more importantly from our point of view, the direction of change toward which the policy has further propelled the national economy.

In this perspective, the first basic point which must be stressed is that in spite of the broad development goals which had been articulated, the main interest of the policy makers and the project administrators appeared to be to raise marketable agricultural production, mainly cereal production, primarily for the benefit of the urban population. In his recent detailed evaluation of CADU, Cohen for example, concluded as follows:

"Despite all the activities spelled out in CADU's annual reports and summarized by the organization charts, the project's principal programs centered on agricultural extension, input distribution, and output marketing..."[16]

And as he had earlier explained: "Social development objectives were never well articulated or translated into clearly justified activity targets."[17]

The writer, however, has stated that it was the "central position of [his] book that CADU-ARDU is a classic example of integrated rural development."[18] An analysis of this key feature of the project is provided in Annex 4.1.

The second important observation which must be made is that the economic outcomes of the various projects considered within the national perspective had been extremely small. The national and international preoccupation with the projects and the wide publicity which was given to them seem to have left the wrong impression in the minds of some people that a substantial part of Ethiopia's subsistence agriculture was being influenced by them. This was far from the truth.

As already stated above, certainly all of the estimated 42,000 peasant producers of Chilalo had been touched by the project as of 1974/75. This number, however, constituted less than 1 percent of the estimated five million rural households in the country at that time. With regard to WADU, it will be recalled that in accordance with its main goal, the project was reported to have resettled only 750 new households between 1970 and 1974. This number of settlers constituted only about 2 percent of the estimated 30,000–32,000 households of Welaita Sub-Region during that period. The ADDP, at least in the beginning, aimed to reach about 13,000 peasant households in Adaa District. This number constituted less than 0.3% of the total rural peasant households in the country as a whole.

The impact of MPP between 1970–71 and 1973–74 was equally unimpressive. Less than 50,000 peasant households had received limited quantities of fertilizer and improved seeds by 1973/74 (Table 4.1). It is quite clear, therefore, that the impact of all the projects on the subsistence sector as a whole was infinitesmal. Indeed, this was a matter which was only too well known to the planners.[19]

Table 4.1 Fertilizer and Improved Seed Distributed Under the MPP — 1970/71–1973/74

Period	Number of Participants	Fertilizer (Quintals)	Improved Seeds (Quintals)
1970/71	4,618	9,460	220
1971/72	12,706	20,200	200
1972/73	25,424	35,167	866
1973/74	49,594	67,239	1,232

Source: *Evaluation of Agricultural Development Projects and the Future Direction of Rural Development*, A Study Committee Report (in Amharic), May, 1980, p. 25.

A third aspect, which seemed to have been of little concern to the policy-makers was the fact that all of the projects were primarily domains of international finance and foreign management. It must be stressed that, of course, no objection is implied here to international cooperation as such. The repercussions of the large amounts of foreign capital and the dominance of foreign influence in the project activities cannot, however, be ignored. The pattern of external dependency which had begun to take root in the country deepened as a result of the projects. The problem was a serious one especially when viewed in the context of a project such as CADU which was found to be too costly to have relevance to the circumstances of Ethiopia. The projects were, moreover, largely externally designed. Aside from the dominance of foreign experts whose knowledge about the problems and needs of Ethiopian rural producers was limited, the projects initiated a top-down approach of development in which the producers had little to contribute save to carry out the instructions of extension agents. Concerning these points, Cohen observed:

> "...There is no question that the design team had not done all the background work needed to understand the Chilalo area...
>
> "...To be sure, CADU/ARDU was a project 'for' rather than 'by' rural people."[20]

This leads us to raise a fourth basic problem concerning the regional and minimum-package projects. The projects were mainly preoccupied with the diffusion of a more-or-less standard package of yield-raising inputs such as fertilizer, improved seeds, pesticides and herbicides. There are many weaknesses of such an approach of development. In the first place, in the case of Ethiopia one often encounters a wide diversity of production conditions even within a relatively limited geographical area, a fact which makes a standard package designed on a "model farm" much less useful to many of the producers than assumed by the project administrators.[21] Furthermore, given the limited number of extension agents, there was not always certainty that the technological prescriptions were applied by the peasants as intended by the "experts." As a result, the returns from the investments in many cases were likely to be less than potentially attainable.

A more fundamental problem arises where there was little relation between the package of inputs prescribed and the actual problems of production which are faced by the farmers. This was found to be sometimes the case on the basis of a survey undertaken in Adaa District where the ADDP was implemented (Table 4.2) Thus, while the producers were encouraged to make use of fertilizers in relatively large numbers, only a small proportion of them regarded the decline of soil fertility as a serious problem. While the problem of pests was regarded as a serious problem by many of the peasants, only a relatively smaller proportion of them were making use of pesticides. As already indicated above, there was also no certainty that the inputs were actually applied

Table 4.2 An Example of the Incongruence Between Production Problems and Technological Inputs

1. Problems of Agricultural Production As Perceived by the Peasantry of ADAA

Problems	Respondents Ranking Problems as (1) and (2)	
	Number	Percent of Respondents
Pests	191	64.8
Weeds	171	58.0
Wild Animals	113	38.3
Climatic Variation	44	14.9
Decline in Soil Fertility	21	7.2
Others	10	3.4

2. Extent of Usage of Selected Inputs by the Same Group of Respondents

Inputs	Number	Percent of Respondents
Fertilizer	203	68.8
"Improved" seeds	38	12.9
Pesticides	60	20.3
Herbicides	21	7.1

Source: Fassil G. Kiros, "Search for Alternatives of Agricultural Development Strategy Under Varied Conditions of Peasant Production in Ethiopia — A Case Study in Adaa *Wereda*", *Ethiopian Journal of Agricultural Sciences.* Vol. 2, No. 2, (June 1980), p. 119.

in the correct manner. One other study undertaken in another district, for example, found out the following situation:

"The scientists recommended 125 kgs of DAP and 73 kgs of Urea per hectare. The rate of fertilizer used per hectare by the peasants on the rest of their communal farms varied. They were 13 kgs for Misrak, 40 kgs for Ilala Gojo, 93 kgs for Welmera Chokie, 44 kgs for Welmera Goro, and 125 kgs of DAP for Markos. Compared to the recommended rates this is about 10.4% for Misrak, 32% for Ilala Gojo, 74.4 for Welmera Chokie and 35.2% for Welmera Goro. This phenonomen also applies for the seed rate used for wheat and barley... "[22]

In this relation, the author has reported elsewhere the following rather amusing exchange which he overheard between two peasants:

Peasant 1: "Was the pesticide you sprayed enough"?

Peasant 2: "No, I sprayed it thinly."

During another field study, when the author asked a peasant which types of fertilizer he normally applied, he responded: "Why, of course, the one which makes for more 'seeds'; the other type is for the 'leaves'." These incidents primarily reflect the weakness of the extension services.

A fifth and even more basic problem concerns the limited potential of "sustainability" of the green-revolution strategy which was initiated in Ethiopia. Leaving aside the question of technical relevance raised above, it must be recognized that none of the main inputs prescribed, including chemical fertilizer, pesticides and herbicides are produced in Ethiopia. These are inputs which would need to be all imported, and in ever increasing quantities if they are to be made available to increasing numbers of producers. Indeed, the rapidly rising prices of energy-dependent inputs such as fertilizer have already rendered such inputs unattainable by the vast majority of the producers (Table 4.3). One of the studies cited above, for instance, found that over 60%

of the peasants interviewed had to discontinue the use of chemical fertilizers because of their inability to purchase such inputs.[23] This is, however, not to imply that the imported inputs actually constitute the technology appropriate in all cases of peasant production in Ethiopia.

Table 4.3   Trend of Increase in the Average Price of DAP and Urea in Ethiopia

Year	Birr Per Quintal
1976/77	44
1977/78	44
1978/79	55
1979/80	65
1980/81	85
1981/82	100

Source: *Major Problems of Grain Production and Marketing and Proposed Policy Measure*, (Report in Amharic). Working Group of Staff of Office of National Committee for Central Planning, Agricultural Marketing Corporation, Ministry of Domestic Trade and Ministry of Agriculture, Sept. 1983, Annex 8.

The problem of sustainability of the production technology had manifested itself even in connection with the new seed varieties which had been "adopted" by many peasants within the country. Many of the new seed varieties released for use by the peasants have had to be abandoned, sometimes because they tended to lose their viability in a relatively short time for one reason or another (Table 4.4). This indicates the limited research capability to produce a range of sustainable varieties suited to the production conditions which prevail in particular localities. It was, moreover, found that the application of a few of the "improved" seed varieties tended to create new production problems. For example, two of the new wheat varieties, Laketch and Supremo, being short-strawed, were found to be vulnerable to weed competition, and this under the conditions where the application of fertilizer tended to increase weed infestation. Greater numbers of man-hours were, therefore, required to control weeds as well as to harvest the new short-stemmed varieties or plants.

A more basic concern has also been raised regarding the appropriateness of altering the genetic characteristics of particular seeds under conditions in which a complex system of multiple crop production prevails. Thus, according to one scientist:

"The structural and functional complexity of the Ethiopian agricultural system is assumed, by the present author, to result in its stability or homeostasis compared to most specialized ecosystems. It thus deserves critical attention for the contribution to modern plant breeding theories in general, and specifically for the application, regionally, of specific polycultural breeding strategies in a country like Ethiopia, particularly where there are several indications of unsuccessfulness and failures of the monocultural breeding strategy."[24]

The potential danger indicated by the tendency toward monocultural practices in the circumstances of peasant production which is perpetually threatened by high risks of crop failures due to many causes is obvious enough.

Table 4.4 Wheat Varieties Released and Later Abandoned by CADU 1967–1983

Variety	Year of Release	Reason for Abandonment
Kenya	1967	Stripe and stem rust
Mayo 48	1968	Stem rust
Yaktana 54	1968	" "
Salmoyo	1969	" "
Supremo	1969	" "
Romany	1970	" "
Laketch	1970	" "
K. Kanga	1971	Leaf blotch
K. Mamba	1970	Stripe rust

Source: T. Nichola, *Agricultural Research and Extension in Ethiopia: The State of the Art*, IDR Research Report No. 22, Addis Ababa University, March 1985, p. 31.

Thus, basic changes in the prevailing production system would obviously necessitate a holistic and long-term development approach based on an appreciation of the prevailing sociopolitical and agroecological circumstances. This is, however, perhaps to expect too much from projects whose primary purpose was to raise as much production as the land could yield without introducing any basic changes to the structural features of the system of production by which it was fettered.

CONCLUSION

It should be noted in concluding this chapter that, in spite of the many problems associated with the comprehensive and minimum package projects, it could not be denied that they did serve, to some extent and at whatever cost, to raise the much desired marketable food-grain production for the benefit of the urban population. The overall impact of the policy of agricultural modernization was, however, to increase and accelerate the historical processes which were outlined in the preceding chapter. For, this new policy not only turned out to be yet another burden on many rural producers, and a threat to many more, but also increased the level of external dependency of the economy more than had been experienced before.

It may be argued that the importation of foreign investment, technology and expertise was inevitable given the general backwardness of the Ethiopian economy at the time. The point is not, however, that foreign technology or investment ought to have been avoided. It is rather that there was little possibility for a policy which was based on the total dependence on the importation of the most essential inputs to advance much farther than it did, and perhaps more basically, that there appeared to be little thought given as to where it would all eventually lead.

Annexes to Chapter 4

Annex 4.1 The Application of the Concept of Integrated Development by ARDU

The evidence available does not seem to indicate that a clearly established concept of "integrated rural development" has been evolved in CADU or ARDU.[1]

It is proposed that at least [five] dimensions of the concept of "integration" could be recognized... The first dimension suggested pertains to the relationship of rural development to national development generally. The purpose of integration in this respect is to ensure that rural development is dynamically linked with the national development strategy.

The second dimension pertains to integration on the organizational level. It is obvious that within the sphere of rural development, many governmental and popular organizations have various roles to play. There is also the familiar problem of establishing effective linkage between research and extension activities. How can coordination be achieved in these areas so that such development activities can be made to reinforce one another? What instruments of coordination are available for this purpose? Such are the types of questions to be answered in regard to the organizational aspect of integration.

A third aspect of the problem of integration has to do with the relationship among the objectives of particular projects. It calls attention to the need for avoiding conflicts and contradictions in the design and application of particular rural development activities. How do particular measures relate to each other? How do they affect particular communities? What possible side-effects might they entail? These are the types of questions to be raised in this respect.

The intertemporal coordination of the sequence of development measures constitutes [a fourth] dimension of integration....

The final aspect of integration concerns the substantive inputs and measures designed and applied in response to the set of demands identified in particular rural communities. This is the aspect of integration with which the CADU/ARDU project have been primarily concerned.

Considering the last one first, in order to make a fair assessment of the degree of application of the integrated approach of development as seems to have been understood at Arsi, it was felt necessary to identify those elements of a "package" which may have relatively more relevance than others to most of the rural communities. The elements chosen as regards farm inputs are fertilizer, improved seeds, and farm implements. From among the other types of activities, potable water supply was selected as being more-or-less equally needed in most communities. The evidence available suggests that these elements do not feature as common elements of any development "package" applied within Arsi Region.

According to one sample survey recently undertaken, expenditures of the peasants in the various communities on fertilizer and improved seeds vary widely. Thus within Chilalo, Bekoji peasants were reported to spend nearly Birr 75.00 on fertilizer annually on the average whereas several other communities spent less than one half that amount. Bekoji peasants also spent on the average nearly Birr 9.00 per annum on improved seed, whereas three communities spent less than one-half this amount and three others spent none at all according to the survey.[2] Similar differences can be observed in Arbagugu and Ticho. Of course, it may be argued, but within limits, that the variation in the expenditures may be explained by the differences in agro-ecological and economic conditions. (Some of the variations in the expenditures on fertilizer can, however, be explained by other factors. Studies have shown for example that the application of fertilizer *inter alia* is limited by its relatively high cost.... This may imply that the lower the level of income the less likely the purchase of fertilizer)...

With regard to farm implements an earlier study on CADU had also stated as follows:

"None of the innovations has been as successful as was originally envisaged. Certainly their rate of adoption has not approached that at which Chilalo farmers have availed themselves of fertilizer and improved seed sold by CADU.... Sales of CADU implements have been very limited, while the threshing service has at least until very recently, reached very few farmers and has failed to cover costs."[3]

Further inference about the uneven pattern of the application of the "package" approach can be made from the types and magnitudes of self-help activities promoted in Arsi... Still better indication of the situation in this respect can be obtained by an assessment of the extent to which access to safe drinking water has been provided to the peasantry. The distribution of water supply projects undertaken appears to have been highly uneven. In fact, according to the sample survey already referred to, only a relatively limited number of the peasantry in Chilalo obtain their drinking water from safe sources, the majority reporting that they obtained their drinking water from rivers.

The foregoing findings do not suggest that there has been any systematic application of the "integrated" approach of development in

Arsi with particular reference to the application of substantive inputs and measures.

It would be correct to state that the emphasis of CADU/ARDU has been on the regional or spatial diffusion of inputs. There is little evidence of the deepening and widening of rural change based on intertemporally integrated long-term, medium-term and short-term plans. The latter process would involve the increasing diversification and specialization of production, fuller utilization of human and natural resources, the creation of the conditions for the systematic process for internalizing technological knowhow into productive processes, and the conscious effort to capitalize on experience and the varying circumstances which manifest themselves. It is recognized, of course, that this could be shown to be outside the scope of the ARDU project. The point is that it ought not to have been and ought not to remain so if rural transformation is to be increasingly realized.

It was not possible, based on interviews with officials, to discern readily any conflicts or contradictions between the objectives on elements of the inputs of the ARDU project... It should be noted, however, that studies undertaken in the past on the CADU project have shown that the effect of certain agricultural inputs such as fertilizer was to aggravate certain production problems. A specific instance is the increased weed infestation on fields as a result of the application of fertilizer.

The problem of organizational integration between research and extension does not seem to arise in Arsi as both are part of a single project. This is not to imply, however, that the functions of extension are carried out satisfactorily in all respects. It must also be recognized that the problem of research-extension linkage continues to be a serious problem on the national level.

Finally, it was found through discussions with the appropriate officials that, except perhaps since very recently, it was not possible to appreciate how ARDU fits into the scheme of national, rural or agricultural development.

There was lack of integration of ARDU with other national and regional centers. There could therefore also be expected little coordination to occur in the sphere of planning. Interactions in the course of carrying out development activities were, however, not as rare.

Excerpts from Fassil G. Kiros, "Learning from ARDU — Toward a Regional System of Rural Development in Ethiopia", *Regional Planning and Development in Ethiopia* I, P. Treuner, K.M. Taddese and M. Teshome, (Eds.), Institute of Development Research, Addis Ababa University and IREUS, Stuttgart University, 1985, pp. 199–225.

References and Notes to Annex 4.1

1. The main difference between Chilalo Agricultural Development Unit (CADU) and Arsi Rural Development Unit (ARDU) was that the former was limited to Chilalo Sub-region while the latter covered the entire Arsi Region. It could also be inferred from the goals adopted that ARDU was a more "comprehensive" project than CADU.
2. *Investigations on the Impact of the Agrarian Reform on Peasants' Income and Expenditure Patterns, 1980,* ARDU Publication No. 18, Planning Evaluation and Budget Section, ARDU, Asela, October, 1981, p. 81.
3. G.J. Gill, *Farm Technology Pilot Survey* Research Report, IDR, Addis Ababa University, 1976, p. 2.
4. G.J. Gill, *op. cit.*, p. 125.

References and Notes to Chapter 4

1. Refer for example to Richard Pankhurst, *Economic History of Ethiopia, 1800–1935* (Addis Ababa: Haile Selassie I University Press, 1968), pp. 208–209.
2. Refer to Fassil G. Kiros, *A Review and Analysis of Food and Agricultural Policy in Ethiopia*. A Study Report Submitted to the Organization for Social Science Research in Eastern Africa (OSSREA), (Addis Ababa, January 1986); Fassil G. Kiros, "Learning from ARDU — Toward a Regional System of Rural Development in Ethiopia", *op. cit.*, pp. 199–225. Parts of this Chapter draw from these sources.
3. Arsi Rural Development Unit, Plan for 1976–80, *ARDU Publication* No. 1, (Asela, February 1976), p. 1.
4. According to one study, the internal rate of return to research undertaken by CADU is estimated to be relatively high. Refer to T. Nichola, "Social Returns from Research and Extension Costs in Wheat and Barley in Arsi Region of Ethiopia," Unpublished Master's Dissertation Submitted to the Graduate School, Addis Ababa University, 1985.
5. *Ibid.* p. 95.
6. Arsi Rural Development Unit, Plan for 1976–80, *op. cit.*, pp. 3–5.
7. Refer to Tesfai Tecle, *The Evolution of Alternative Rural Development Strategies in Ethiopia:Implications for Employment and Income Distribution*, (Institute of Development Research, Addis Ababa University, Addis Ababa, and Department of Agricultural Economics, Michigan State University, East Lansing, 1975).
8. *Ibid.*
9. *Ibid.*
10. Provisional Military Administrative Council, *Evaluations of Agricultural Development Projects and the Future Direction of Rural Development*, A Study Committee Report

(in Amharic), (Addis Ababa, May, 1980), p. 25.

11. Refer for example to the various Annual Reports and Study and Evaluation Reports issued by CADU, Work Program and other reports of EPID, and periodic evaluation reports such as the *Final Report on the Appraisal of CADU and EPID* by the Evaluation Team jointly appointed by the Ethiopian Government and SIDA, 1974; *Evaluation of Arsi Rural Development Unit* (Uppsala, 1980, etc.).

12. Refer for instance to Michael Stahl, *Ethiopia: Political Contradictions in Agricultural Development*, (Political Science Association, Uppsala, 67, 1974); Henock Kifle, *Program 1968/69–1970/71 and The Impact on Income Distribution*. CADU Publication No. 66 (August, 1971); Henock Kifle, *Investigation on Mechanized Farming and its Effects on Peasant Agriculture* (1972); John M. Cohen, "Effects of Green Revolution Strategies on Tenants and Small Scale Landowners in Chilalo Region of Ethiopia" *The Journal of Developing Areas,* Vol. 9, No. 3, April, 1975.

13. Refer for example to Keith Griffin, *The Political Economy of Agrarian Change: An Essay on the Green Revolution*, (Cambridge: Harvard University Press, 1974); Harry M. Cleaver, "The Contributions of the Green Revolution", *American Economic Review,* 72, (May 1972), pp. 177–188; Andrew Pearse, *Seeds of Plenty, Seeds of Want, Social and Economic Implications of the Green Revolution*, (Oxford: Clarendon Press, 1980); Vernon W. Ruttan, "The Green Revolution: Seven Generalizations", *International Development*, Vol. XIX, No. 4, (1977), pp. 16–20.

14. Ruttan, *op. cit.*, p. 20.

15. John M. Cohen, "Land Tenure and Rural Development in Africa", in *Agricultural Development in Africa*, Robert H. Bates and Michael Lofchie, (Eds.), (Berkeley and Los Angeles: University of California Press, 1960), pp. 366–367.

16. John M. Cohen, *Integrated Rural Development, The Ethiopian Experience and the Debate*, (The Scandinavian Institute of African Studies, Uppsala, 1987), p. 74.
17. *Ibid.*, p. 81.
18. *Ibid.*, p. 31.
19. Refer to Imperial Ethiopian Government, *Third Five Year Development Plan, op. cit.*, pp. 190–193.
20. *Integrated Rural Development, The Ethiopian Experience and the Debate, op. cit.*, pp. 246, 249.
21. For detailed discussions of these problems refer to Fassil G. Kiros, "Search for Alternatives of Agricultural Development Strategy Under Varied Conditions of Peasant Production in Ethiopia — A Case Study in Adaa *Wereda*, *Ethiopian Journal of Agricultural Sciences*, Vol. 2, No. 2, (1980); and Fassil G. Kiros, "Learning from ARDU — Toward a Regional System of Rural Development in Ethiopia", in *Regional Planning and Development in Ethiopia 1, op. cit.*, pp. 199–225.
22. Tewolde Berhan G. Egziabher *et al.*, *Participation of a Rural Community in the Identification of Technological Problems in Ethiopia (A Case Study from Welmera Wereda)*, Ethiopian Science and Technology Commission, United Nations University and IDRC, Addis Ababa, Dec. 1980, p. 50.
23. "Search for Alternatives of Agricultural Development Strategy ....", *op. cit.* p. 123.
24. Endashaw Bekele, "Analysis of Regional Patterns of Phenotypic Diversity in the Ethiopian Tetraploid and Hexaploid Wheats", *Hereditas*, Vol. 101, No. 132, (1984).

The Policy of Revolutionary Transformation of Agriculture _____

INTRODUCTION

The aim of this chapter is to highlight some of the most important revolutionary policies and economic strategies which were pursued since 1975 particularly in the rural sector. An attempt will then be made in the following chapter to make an assessment of the impacts of the new policies and measures.

In the period prior to 1974, most students of Ethiopian affairs agreed that the main shackle on the development of the national economy was the archaic landholding system which prevailed. Few, if any, anticipated the revolutionary outburst of 1974, much less the course of events which followed that period. There was little doubt that the winds of political change were gathering momentum at least since the mid-1960s when university students first carried the slogan "land to the tiller" in the streets of Addis Ababa. As already noted, the student movement received impetus when the contradictions which appeared as a result of the implementation of the policy of agricultural modernization caught their attention and those of other progressive elements in the society. Paradoxically, therefore, a policy which basically sought to maintain the traditional *status quo* was to bring forth a policy of the revolutionary transformation of society. It was, moreover, significant that a powerful trigger of the 1974 revolution happened to be the famine in Wello, for that event represented a manifestation of the crisis of subsistence which resulted from the cumulative effects of the socio-political processes discussed in the preceding chapters. We must hasten to add, however, that it would be too simplistic to attribute the revolutionary changes to any isolated events. Whatever the proximate causes, the revolutionary outburst clearly reflected the culmination of social and political contradictions of much larger scale and dimensions.

Many writers have placed the Ethiopian revolution among the most radical to be found within the third-world countries of Africa and elsewhere.[1] At the same time, a number have argued that the forces which have shaped the Ethiopian revolution were quite different from those in the other countries. Halliday and Molyneux, for example, have argued as follows:

> "In a comparative perspective, the Ethiopian revolution of 1974 would appear to have little in common with most other recent Third World social upheavals... The Ethiopian revolution was reminiscent not of the recent upsurges in the Third World but of the classic revolutions of Europe — France in 1789 and the February 1917 revolution in Russia — and it took place in a country displaying many of the features of these two societies on the eve of their revolutions. The transition to capitalism was far from complete, but it had already weakened the traditional bases of social and political power. *This transition, combined with a protracted agrarian crisis, was forcing ever-greater sections of the peasantry into destitution and the agrarian crisis*

was depriving other sectors of the economy of the resources needed for expansion..."[2] (Italics added).

According to these writers, external forces played a relatively minor role in shaping the revolutionary movement in Ethiopia. They remind us that revolutionary movements which took place in other parts of Africa (Angola, Mozambique, Guinea-Bissau and Zimbabwe) and Indo-China (Vietnam, Cambodia, Laos) developed in the context of anti-colonial struggles.

It must readily be admitted that the Ethiopian experience has been unique in a number of respects. One is, however, hardly justified to underestimate the role played by international economic and political forces in shaping the course of events in Ethiopia. As explained in the preceding chapters, the modernization policy pursued in the country was ultimately tied to external economic and political circumstances. Indeed, the authors cited above have acknowledged that the transition to capitalism in Ethiopia was "an exogeneously powered transition."[3] The contradictions which arose out of the policy of modernization have contributed significantly to the revolutionary changes which occurred in the country. It is also important to remember that Ethiopia still continues to be subjected to the same external forces afflicting those African countries which have only recently escaped the yoke of colonialism.

The background of the Ethiopian revolution has, however, yet to be brought into full perspective. Of equally important interest is a better understanding of how it was that the revolution came to take a most radical course, perhaps no less radical than any experienced elsewhere. We must leave these difficult tasks to the political analysts and historians.

THE 1975 RURAL LANDS PROCLAMATION

Among the most important outcomes of "socialist-oriented" revolutions are the introduction of agrarian reform and the "socialization" of production in the agricultural sector. It is on these basic aspects that we focus attention in the first part of the chapter. The discussions of this and the next chapter cover the period up to the overthrow of the revolutionary regime.

The first and most important reform measure undertaken by the Provisional Military Administrative Council (PMAC) after it took power was the 1975 Proclamation to Provide for the Public Ownership of Rural Lands. The Proclamation came as a direct response to the loud cry of "land to the tiller", or so at least its rhetoric sounded. Its preamble proclaimed:

> "Whereas, in countries like Ethiopia where the economy is agricultural a person's right, honour, status and standard of living is determined by his relation to the land...;
>
> Whereas, the development of Ethiopia of the future can be assured not by permitting the exploitation of the many by the few as is now the case, but only by instituting basic change in agrarian relations which would lay the basis upon which, through work by cooperation, the development of one becomes the development of all...;
>
> Whereas, it is necessary to distribute land, increase rural income, and thereby lay the basis for the expansion of industry and the growth of the economy by providing for the participation of the peasantry in the national market;
>
> Whereas, it is essential to abolish the feudal system in order to release for industry the human labour suppressed within such system;
>
> Whereas, it is necessary to narrow the gap in rural wealth and incomes;
>
> Now, therefore, ...it is hereby proclaimed to provide for the public ownership of rural lands."[4]

This Proclamation is a landmark in Ethiopia's recent history although, as we shall see, its full benefits were not to be realized due to policies subsequently adopted by the Government. It swept away all at once the maze of landholding systems which had prevailed in the country for centuries. When in the past a single landowner or absentee landlord could claim thousands of hectares of agricultural land, all rural land was rendered the collective property of all Ethiopians, and individuals could have use rights to as much as 10 hectares of agricultural land. Not only was tenancy abolished, but also the use of hired labor in agriculture was prohibited except under special circumstances. Land, in other words, was to belong to those who would till it themselves.

The Proclamation provided for the creation of peasant associations consisting of all peasant households within an area of 800 hectares. The land was then to be distributed by each peasant association to its members. Initially, the participants of the Development-Through-Cooperation Campaign *(Zemecha)* played the key role in defining the areas to be covered by particular peasant associations, and in land distribution. In some cases, the participant students discouraged land distribution and tried to promote its collective cultivation. This, however, did not last long.

The Process of Land Distribution

There has been no nation-wide study undertaken to assess the implementation of the 1975 Proclamation. It should be obvious that the introduction of a more-or-less uniform agrarian policy under the highly varied conditions which characterize rural Ethiopia could lead to potential problems of implementation. A study should have been justified also because of the initial haphazard process in which the Proclamation was implemented. Sample studies have, however, endeavored to describe the process of implementation and the problems of land distribution which have occurred in different parts of the country.[5] Examples of what appear to be relatively common practices of land distribution are discussed below.

As would be expected, the general practice of peasant associations was to distribute all the available stock of cultivable land to their members. However, while the land stock was fixed in size, the potential number of claimants to the land would tend to continually increase because of the number of young people who come of age (18 years old) to be entitled to land. All the land having been initially distributed, the problem would, therefore, arise as to how to provide for the new members of the peasant associations. One solution was to redistribute the entire stock of land by the increased number of producers. This practice was quite common until it came to be discouraged. The likely consequences of this and other practices will be considered in the next chapter.

Another practice pertained to the desire on the part of the peasantry to achieve a degree of equity in land distribution. The issues which had to be faced in this case were firstly, how to distribute the land which generally consisted of uneven levels of quality, and secondly how to allot land equitably among the different households the number of members of which varied relatively widely.

A common solution to the first problem was to allocate a share of land of each level of quality to each household, a process which generally resulted in at least three plots — "fertile", "moderately fertile", and "relatively infertile" (more-or-less corresponding to the traditional pattern of the quality distribution of land as *lem, lemtef,* and *teff*). A common solution to the second problem was to distribute land in accordance with family size which meant the expansion of existing holdings of households or the addition of new plots as households claimed their entitlements because of increasing numbers of dependents. The practice of distributing land according to family size tended in some cases to contribute to the increase of the number of plots cultivated by each household.[6]

Given these and other practices of land distribution, the pattern of landholdings which emerged turned out to be relatively uneven throughout the country. The size distribution of land varied widely within particular peasant associations, between peasant associations within a particular *wereda*, as well as between administrative regions. The size variation of household landholdings within particular peasant associations reflected the practice of land distribution based on the number of members of every household. Studies have shown that the sizes of landholding within a particular peasant association could range between less than one-quarter of a hectare and six hectares or more.[7]

The variations in average landholdings between peasant associations in a given *wereda* also tended to be relatively large.[8] This was to be expected given the fact that the density of population within the peasant association areas (theoretically 800 hectares each) could vary widely.

The differences in population density also accounted for the differences in the size distribution of land between various regions. This could readily be inferred from the differences in the average number of members of peasant associations in the various regions. For example, in 1987/88, the average size of peasant association members of Wello was found to be over 3 times that of Wellega (Table 5.1). It must, however, be indicated that the average size of landholding which may be obtained from the figures in the table, being based on an assumed 800 hectares of land per peasant association, may not correspond to the actual situation. This is mainly due to the fact that the total size of land in many peasant associations is often smaller than the figure stipulated in the Proclamation. It should be noted, moreover, that the number of peasant associations has tended to fluctuate for various reasons. The numbers in Tigray and Eritrea, for example, declined in later years due to the political situation in these regions. However, except for the nomadic population and those population groups in the remote areas of the country, all rural producers in time were said to have been organized into peasant associations.[9]

The foregoing descriptions only show the overall pattern of land distribution among the peasant population since 1975. It is of course a matter taken for granted that agricutural land is no longer concentrated in the hands of the privileged few. Indeed, even the legal ceiling of 10 hectares stipulated in the Proclamation is rarely reached. While therefore, the goal of equity in land distribution was met to a reasonable degree, it remained to be shown whether the new pattern of landholding would permit its more efficient utilization. We shall address this basic question in the next chapter.

Table 5.1 Average Number of Peasant Associations and Members Under Ministry of Agriculture by Region — 1987/88

Region	Number of Peasant Associations	Total Number of Members	Estimated Average Number of Members per Peasant Association
Arsi	1,027	241,986	236
Bale	589	114,624	195
Eritrea	471	111,640	237
Gamo Gofa	803	209,982	261
Gojjam	1,770	563,307	318
Gondar	1,063	391,115	368
Harerghe	950	279,047	294
Illubabor	564	104,111	185
Kefa	973	228,994	235
Shewa	5,352	1,382,500	258
Sidamo	1,057	373,524	353
Tigray	51	27,564	540
Wellega	1,510	247,270	163
Wello	1,225	648,992	530
Total	17,405	4,924,656	283

Source: *Ministry of Agriculture, Annual Report of Cooperative Organization Division* (in Amharic), (Addis Ababa, June 1988), p. 29.

THE CREATION OF RURAL MASS ORGANIZATIONS

The impact of the Ethiopian agrarian reform, and indeed of the revolutionary changes as a whole, can only be appreciated by the consideration of the new institutional arrangements. The institutions which were created since 1975 in the political and economic domains were many and were all-encompassing. This can be appreciated by the consideration of the new institutional arrangements in the agricultural sector alone. The new institutions fell into two broad categories, namely the government agencies and the mass organizations. Superimposed on these or perhaps embedded in them were the political and control bodies.

Where there was a single ministry in the agricultural sector in the pre-1975 period, three such ministries were created. The first of these was the Ministry of Agriculture proper, which had the responsibility for policy formulation, planning and development of the peasant sector. The second was the Ministry of State Farm Development which was created in 1980. This Ministry had the responsibility of organizing and promoting the development of large-scale commercial farms. The third Ministry, which was also established in 1980, was the Ministry of Coffee and Tea Development. The main responsibility of this Ministry was the promotion of coffee production, and to a limited extent that of tea production as well. These ministries were organized horizontally and vertically resulting in the creation of numerous responsibility centers operating throughout the country.

In addition to the three ministries, semi-autonomous agencies were also created which operated within the rural sector. Among these were the Relief and Rehabilitation Commission (RRC) and the Agricultural Marketing Corporation (AMC). Although RRC was created with the primary responsibility of relief work, it actually became an agency which was involved in development activities as part of its rehabilitation program. This agency has been no less prominent than any of the other agencies operating in the rural sector.

The AMC was the agency responsible for the purchase and distribution of agricultural produce throughout the country. As will be discussed in the next chapter, few institutions have been the subject of as much criticism as the AMC.

The mass organizations of primary interest here are the peasant associations and the service and producers' cooperatives. (This, however is not to underestimate the role of women and youths associations or other groups which operated under the auspices of the peasant associations). In the following pages, we consider first the basic rural mass organizations and the "planned" process of their transformation into producers' cooperatives. This will then be followed by a discussion of the objectives and activities of the alternative agricultural organizations, namely the state farms.

The Transitional Rural Institutions — The Peasant Associations and Service Cooperatives

The discussions which follow are based on the situation which prevailed as of early 1990.

Few institutions have affected the economic, political and social life of Ethiopians since 1975 more than the peasant associations and their counterparts in the urban areas, the urban dwellers' associations. The peasant associations in particular were assigned wide-ranging responsibilities and operated with a relative degree of local autonomy particularly in matters of land distribution and adjudication of conflicts among their members. However, no nation-wide study has been undertaken to assess the extent to and the manner in which the peasant associations have been able to fulfill their assigned responsibilities (Annex 5.1). As might be expected, the effectiveness of these institutions in carrying out their tasks tended to vary.

The peasant associations were most instrumental in implementing specific government directives, which were economic or political in nature. It is important to note in this relation that the associations were organized hierarchically up to the national level, with their highest organ, the All-Ethiopian Peasant Association (AEPA) being located in Addis Ababa.

If the peasant associations were assigned political as well as economic responsibilities, their service cooperatives were primarily economic organizations. The range of economic responsibilities of service cooperatives was very wide (Annex 5.2). A service cooperative could be created by a minimum of three and a maximum of ten peasant associations within a rural area. This, therefore, rendered its area of operation much wider than the peasant associations. The number of service cooperatives, their membership and other particualrs are shown in Annex 5.3. Over 90% of all peasant associations had already become members of service cooperatives by the late 1980s.

The most important activities undertaken by the service cooperatives included the supply of some basic consumption manufactures which were needed by the peasantry, the supply of agricultural inputs such as fertilizers, the marketing of agricultural produce as an intermediary between the peasants and the Agricultural Marketing Corporation, and the provision of flourmill and grain storage services. Some schools and clinics were also reported to have been built by the service cooperatives.[10]

In spite of the dominance and wide-ranging activities of the peasant associations and service cooperatives, they were both considered as transitional rural organizations as explained in the 1979 Policy on Agricultural Producers' Cooperatives.[11] This Policy provided a detailed explanation of the gradual process of transformation of the transitional organizations into the planned future institutions — the agricultural producers' cooperatives (APCs). The APCs are discussed in more detail below as they were regarded by the regime as the foundation of its agrarian "socialist" plan.

The Plan for the Development of Agricultural Producers' Cooperatives

The central aim of agricultural producers' cooperatives was proclaimed to be to attain control of the means of production in agriculture thereby *inter alia:*

> "to increase agricultural production by making use of modern technology and by consolidating the small and fragmented holdings... to promote and establish socialist conditions in rural areas and to safeguard the political and social interests of the peasantry; [and] to create the conditions appropriate for facilitating planned development..."[12]

Three stages were distinguished in the development of agricultural producers' cooperatives, namely the *malba, welba*, and *weland*. These three terms, it may be noted, were coined anew by the policy-makers. They may be taken as being analogous to the Orwellian "newspeak" as manifested in the Ethiopian experiment.

A *malba* was defined as a first-stage APC. It would come into being:

1. When farm-land except for up to one-fifth of a hectare left for individual cultivation, would become collective property;
2. When the members of the cooperative would allow the use of implements and draught animals for cooperative production; and
3. When distribution of income would be based on the following bases:
   (a) According to work contributed to the cooperative; and
   (b) According to implements and draught animals made available on rent to the cooperative.

A *malba* was, therefore, similar to the Stage I cooperative (LPG) of the former German Democratic Republic or to the higher stage agricultural producers' cooperatives (APC) of the People's Republic of China.

A *welba* would come into being when the following conditions would be fulfilled:

1. All land made collective property (but up to one-tenth left for individual use);
2. All implements and draught animals made cooperative property; and
3. Distribution would be based according to the socialist principle: "from each according to his ability to each according to his work."

A *weland* was envisaged to be an enlarged advanced producers' cooperative to be established under the following conditions:

1. All land of several *welbas* and their other means of production to be brought under its control (the average land size to be 4,000 hectares and the membership of 500 farmers); and
2. The members of each *welba* to be converted into members of a *habre* (roughly brigade) of the *weland*.

The *weland* may somewhat resemble the commune of the People's Republic of China. Its emergence would mark the attainment of advanced technological development based on large-scale production in agriculture.

The Policy provided for four alternative models leading from the stage of peasant association to the stage of *welba*. It also explained how the service cooperative would gradually be transformed into a *weland*. A peasant association could be transformed directly into a *welba* if the members so desired and otherwise fulfilled the policy prerequisites. Alternatively, a *welba* could be created by some peasants within a peasant association area and gradually increase its membership until it encompassed the entire association. A peasant association could also be entirely converted into a *malba* by a single step and then into a *welba*. Finally, a peasant association could gradually be transformed into a *malba* and then in time converted into a *welba*. The latter approach would be the one more consistent with the gradual process of development of producers' cooperatives envisaged by the policy.

The creation of the *weland* would involve something of a metamorphosis in which the service cooperative would become an "association of producers' cooperative" if most of its members (the peasant associations) became *welbas* and decided to form a *weland*. Once the *weland* came into being, it would be organized into brigades and work teams.

It was desired that the development of agricultural producers' cooperatives would follow the so-called Lenin's plan which *inter alia* required the voluntary decisions of the peasants themselves to form such cooperatives. However, various incentives were to be provided to the rural producers to form producers' cooperatives. Thus, priority was given to the cooperatives in the provision of credit, and technological and other services. The service cooperatives were required to reserve 25% of their surplus for credits to the producers' cooperatives. Where only some of the members of a peasant association form a producers' cooperative, election to the main offices of the former were reserved for members of the latter. Agricultural producers' cooperatives also benefited from lower taxes as well as greater subsidies than individual producers.

Quite obviously, therefore, the Government placed much emphasis on the promotion of agricultural producers' cooperatives at least until 1990. In fact, few other policies in the agricultural sector received as much emphasis as the promotion of these cooperatives. However, as we shall see, the actual result achieved in this area was very limited.

THE CREATION OF STATE FARMS

The Government had also placed emphasis on the promotion of State agricultural enterprises. We consider below the objectives and structure of this state sector.

The State farm sector came into being following the 1975 agrarian reform Proclamation when the Government undertook responsibility for the management of commercial farms which were nationalized. The objectives of the Ministry of State Farms were described as follows:

"to alleviate the country's food problems; produce adequate amount of raw materials for industry; expand output for foreign exchange earning; expand establishment of agro-industries; create employment opportunities."[13]

The organization of the State farm sector underwent a number of changes. Broadly, the organizational structure consisted of the headquarters of the Ministry and a number of regional and specialized agencies. The regional centers consisted of three corporations, namely the Northwestern, Southern, and Awash Agricultural Development Corporations. Each one of these agencies was further organizationally subdivided down to the farm level. The corporations which performed specialized functions were the Horticultural Corporation, Livestock and Meat Corporation, Agricultural Equipment and Technical Services Corporation, and Ethiopian Seed Corporation. Each of these corporations was a semi-autonomous agency with responsibility to the Ministry of State Farm Development.

The land area cultivated by the state farms initially expanded relatively rapidly but later appeared to be stabilized. In spite of the emphasis made on the promotion of state farms, as we shall see, their share in the total area cultivated or their contribution to total production remained to be very small.

It may be noted that the Ministry of Coffee and Tea Development was also engaged in the promotion of state farms. However, nearly all of Ethiopian coffee was actually produced by the peasant sector and the amount of tea production in the country remained quite small. The Ethiopian State farms, as all such organizations in nearly all countries, have been the subject of much debate. We shall, therefore, consider the problem of operation of these organizations in some detail in the next chapter.

AGRICULTURAL PRODUCTION STRATEGY SINCE 1975

The period immediately following the revolutionary outburst was a period of intense political struggle and of national mobilizations against external aggressors and secessionist elements. The country was, therefore, soon faced by a deep economic crisis. The rate of growth of GDP fell to the level of 0.9% by 1977/78 implying a drastic fall in per capita GDP. Hence, no sooner had the political and military confrontations abated than the Government turned its attention to the task of rehabilitating the economy and of raising production especially in the agricultural sector. A mammoth organization, the National Revolutionary Development Campaign and Central Planning Supreme Council (NRDC/CPSC) was set up with responsibility to prepare and implement annual economic plans and to create the conditions for initiating long-term development planning. Six annual plans were prepared and implemented between 1978/79 and 1983/84. The annual plans were quite broad in scope and involved the participation of nearly all of the governmental organizations in their preparation.

The campaign period was succeeded by the launching of the

Ten-Year Perspective Plan covering the period 1984/85 through 1993/94. That Plan was quite comprehensive and aimed at attaining highly ambitious goals in economic, social and political spheres. In the following pages, an attempt is made to highlight the main goals and results of the annual plans as well as those of the Ten-Year Perspective Plan with particular reference to the agricultural sector.

Agriculture in the Six-Years Campaign

The peasant and state farm sectors were the main focus of agricultural production policy during the campaign period.

The production strategy pursued in the peasant sector during this period in large part consisted of the promotion of activities which had been initiated in the pre-revolution period. Of the comprehensive projects, the successor of CADU — Arsi Rural Development Unit (ARDU) — continued to operate in the post-revolution period. The new designation, ARDU, reflected the fact that the project had extended its activities to two other sub-regions of Arsi, namely Ticho and Arbagugu. The objectives and activities of ARDU were similar to those of its predecessor. However, while a few activities were no longer within its scope of responsibility, others appeared to be pursued with a greater degree of emphasis. Among the new responsibilities of ARDU was the promotion of peasant mass organizations. One of its main activities of distributing production inputs was soon taken over by the newly created service cooperatives. In this respect, the operations of ARDU were very similar to those of the minimum-package program.

As indicated in the last chapter, the implemention of the second phase of the minimum package program (MPP II) had been delayed until the early 1980s. However, extension activities were being continued following the completion of the first phase of the program. Indeed, the diffusion of fertilizer and "improved" seeds greatly increased immediately following 1975 (Table 5.2). While the objectives of MPP II were in general similar to those of the first phase, there were differences of emphasis, organization, and channels of distribution of production inputs. As in the case of ARDU, the main emphasis during this period was placed on the promotion of peasant mass organizations, and especially the agricultural producers' cooperatives. The Ministry of Agriculture itself was reorganized at the central level reflecting this new orientation. Emphasis was also placed on strengthening agricultural administration on the *wereda* level, since the aim was to reach most of these districts through teams of extension agents.

The launching of the economic campaign gave impetus to the activities of MPP II as well as ARDU. The distribution of yield-increasing inputs to the peasantry was pursued with vigor through the new mass organizations. It was, however, the agricultural producers' cooperatives, of which only a few had come into being, which were to be given high priority in the supply of the inputs.

Table 5.2 Distribution of Fertilizer and "Improved Seeds" — 1975/76–1977/78

Year	Fertilizer (Quintals)	"Improved" Seeds (Quintals)
1975–76	220,000	10,954
1976–77	250,100	23,465
1977–78	125,711	3,090

Source: *Evaluation of Agricultural Development Projects and the Future Direction of Rural Development, op.cit.*, p. 25.

In accordance with the new Government policy, high priority was given to the establishment and promotion of the activities of State farms. During the campaign period, roughly 40% of the total amount of fertilizer and around 70% of the improved seeds were supplied to these farms which accounted then for only

Table 5.3 Fertilizer Distribution by Major Users — 1978/1979–1982/83 (in Quintals)

Users	1978/79	1979/80	1980/81	1981/82	1982/83
Peasant Associations	335,000	412,000	292,700	291,284	479,393
Producers' Cooperatives	–	–	1,461	10,832	20,585
State Farms	105,100	234,500	355,300	382,700	339,789
Agricultural Research	350	380	400	472	985
Settlement Programs	8,190	41,900	29,046	11,152	45,624
Total	448,640	668,780	678,907	696,440	866,376

Source: T. Teka and T. Nichola, *Rural Poverty Alleviation: The Case of Ethiopia* (Institute of Development Research, Addis Ababa University, 1983), pp. 90–91.

Table 5.4 Quantity of Seeds Distributed by the Ethiopian Seed Corporation (in '000 Quintals)

Year	State Farms	Peasant Sector	Others	Total
1979/80	190	13	6	209
	(91)	(6)	(3)	(100)
1980/81	168	35	20	223
	(75)	(16)	(9)	(100)
1981/82	161	7	21	189
	(85)	(4)	(11)	(100)
1982/83	163	25	15	203
	(80)	(12)	(8)	(100)
1983/84	126	17	15	158
	(80)	(11)	(9)	(100)
1984/85	148	165	70	383
	(39)	(43)	(18)	(100)
1985/86	144	80	167	391
	(37)	(20)	(43)	(100)

Note: Figures in parentheses represent percentages.

Source: Ministry of State Farm Development, *Toward A Strategy for the Development of State Farms in Ethiopia*, Volume I, Main Report, (Addis Ababa, 1986), p. 392.

3.5% of total agricultural production. The peasant sector which contributed around 95% of total production received the rest of the inputs (Tables 5.3 and 5.4). The impact of the production strategy pursued during the campaign period will be discussed in more detail in the next chapter.

Agriculture in the Ten-Year Perspective Plan

As indicated above, following the last year of the campaign, and building on the results and experiences of the annual plans, the Ten-Year Perspective Plan was launched. In the economic sphere, the basic target of the plan was to acheive an average annual growth of 6.5% in real GDP. The sectoral rates of growth projected were 10.8% for industry, 6.9% for services, and 4.3% for agriculture.[14]

The development of agriculture was given high priority by the plan. Among the fundamental goals in this sector was the promotion of agricultural producers' cooperatives. It was projected that by 1993/94, these cooperatives would encompass 52.7% of all peasant households and would account for 48.5% of total cultivated area. By comparison, it was projected that state farms would account for about 6.2% of cultivated area by 1993/94.

Among the main agricultural production strategies to be pursued were the expansion of total area under cultivation *inter alia* through population resettlement programs, the development of irrigation schemes, increased supply of improved agricultural inputs to farmers, etc.[15] As we shall see, in spite of the priority assigned to the development of the agricultural sector, the performance of this sector was far below expectations during the first half of the plan period (1984/85–1988/89).

In the latter part of the 1980s, the Government placed greater emphasis on the objective of raising food production by concentrating agricultural inputs and services by stages in about 180 selected "surplus-producing" *weredas*. This strategy which was to be implemented within the framework of the so-called Peasant Agricultural Development Project (PADEP) was not put into full operation.

In accordance with the development plan, the strategy of population resettlement also received much impetus following the 1984/85 famine. It was reported furthermore that the villagization program was being implemented in high gear during the plan period.[16] Both of these programs were subsequently suspended following the criticisms to which they had been subjected mainly by different groups abroad. Few detailed studies can be found on the population resettlement and villagization activities which had been implemented by *ad hoc* governmental bodies. An overall assessment of their impacts is, however, made in the next chapter.

CONCLUSION

The discussion of this chapter has shown that the policies introduced by the revolutionary regime since 1975 stood in sharp contrast to those which they replaced. This was reflected in the rhetoric, in the grandiose "socialization" schemes and the overambitious economic growth plans which were adopted. However, the benefits to the rural population even of the most fundamental reform introduced, namely the agrarian reform, fell far short of expectations. Indeed, as we shall see in the next chapter, the rural society came to be subjugated under a new monolithic form of political control and exploitation which was introduced as a corollary to the agrarian reform program itself.

Annexes to Chapter 5

Annex 5.1 Powers and Duties of the Peasant Associations

Every peasant association formed at any level shall have the powers and duties to:

1. agitate and coordinate the peasantry to properly implement and follow up the implementation of the Public Ownership of Rural Lands Proclamation No. 31/1975 and other proclamations and directives pertaining to rural areas issued or to be issued by the Revolutionary Government;
2. enable the peasantry of Revolutionary Ethiopia to struggle more actively for the liquidation of reactionary plots and for economic construction by uniting and coordinating its struggle with other mass organizations;
3. in cooperation with those concerned, agitate, educate, coordinate the peasantry and render the necessary assistance thereto with a view to expanding and strengthening agricultural producers' cooperatives which are the bases for social construction in rural areas;
4. agitate, educate and coordinate the peasantry, with a view to liberating it from backwardness, by establishing and strengthening agricultural service cooperatives, increasing production and expanding social services;
5. in cooperation with the appropriate government and mass organizations, coordinate the peasantry and make the necessary efforts for the betterment of the lives of peasants living in lands that are overpopulated or of poor productivity and that of nomads;
6. in cooperation with those concerned, coordinate the peasantry with a view to liberating it from archaic mode of production and backward practices and cultures by advancing its ideological outlook and developing its initiative and thereby enhance productivity; render the necessary assistance thereto;
7. follow-up and supervise the proper tilling and development of cultivable land and the augmentation of production;
8. in cooperation with those concerned, make the necessary participation in the effort to enable the peasantry to gain rapid progress in education, health, transport and similar social services;

9. implement properly directives issued by the appropriate government office concerning the conservation, protection and development of forest and wildlife, make the necessary protection to soil and water resources;
10. in cooperation with those concerned, agitate and coordinate its members and follow up their participation in the effort to conserve and protect historical relics and antiquities of Ethiopia;
11. participate fully in the effort to satisfy the education needs of the peasantry; implement plans devised to this effect by the Government from time to time;
12. devise methods by which sports may be popularized among the peasantry with a view to making the peasantry physically fit, healthier and more productive citizens;
13. make the necessary effort to consolidate further the alliance between the urban working masses and the peasantry;
14. make the necessary effort to secure women their due place in the production process with a view to increasing participation in the development of rural areas;
15. follow directives issued by the Government concerning utilization of land.

Source: Provisional Military Administrative Council, Proclamation No. 223 of 1982, *A Proclamation to Provide for the Consolidation of Peasant Associations* (Addis Ababa).

Annex 5.2 Objectives, Powers and Duties of Service Cooperative Societies

The objectives, powers and duties of a service cooperative society shall include the following:

1. to procure crop expansion services;
2. to market the produce of members at fair prices;
3. to give loans at fair interest rates;
4. to give storage and saving services;
5. to supply consumer goods to the members according to their needs;
6. to give education in socialist philosophy and cooperative work in order to enhance the political consciousness of the peasantry;
7. to supply improved agricultural implements and provide tractor services;
8. to collect contributions;
9. to give flour mills services;
10. to organize craftsmen in order to promote industry;
11. to provide political education with a view to establishing agricultural producers' cooperative societies by forming, promoting and consolidating mutual aid teams like *debo*;
12. to sue and be sued;
13. to draw up its internal regulations.

Source: Provisional Ministry Administrative Council Proclamation No. 71 of 1975, *A Proclamation to Provide for the Organization and Consolidation of Peasant Associations* (Addis Ababa).

Annex 5.3 Number of Service Cooperatives and Their Membership Under the Ministry of Agriculture — 1987/88

Region	Number of Service Cooperatives		Number of Member Peasant Associations	Number of Participating Households
	Total	Registered		
Arsi	158	108	1,026	231,427
Bale	169	73	336	67,885
Eritrea	90	38	406	645,285
Gamo Gofa	134	20	580	141,518
Gojjam	396	283	1,667	432,785
Gondar	242	118	731	203,427
Illubabor	111	27	496	76,935
Harerghe	226	149	876	255,587
Kefa	192	45	903	179,036
Shewa	1,102	458	5,266	1,288,914
Sidamo	170	31	790	204,550
Tigray	11	2	33	15,225
Wellega	293	78	1,459	226,869
Wello	302	109	1,069	473,130
Total	3,596	1,539	15,638	4,439,573

Source: *Annual Report of Cooperative Organization Division, op.cit.,* p. 32.

References and Notes to Chapter 5

1. Refer, for example, to Richard R. Fagen, Carmen Diana Deere, and Jose Luis Corragio, (Eds.), *Transition and Development, Problems of Third World Socialism* (New York: Monthly Review Press, 1986); Crawford Young, *Ideology and Development in Africa*, (New Haven and London: Yale University Press, 1982); David and Marina Ottaway, *Afrocommunism*, (New York: Holmes and Meier Publishers, Inc., 1981).

2. Fred Halliday and Maxine Molyneux, *The Ethiopian Revolution*, (London: Unwin Brothers, 1981), pp. 14–15; refer also to John Markakis and Nega Ayele, *Class and Revolution in Ethiopia*, (Trenton: The Red Sea Press, 1986), p. 68; Marina Ottaway, "Social Classes and Corporate Interests in the Ethiopian Revolution", *The Journal of Modern African Studies,* Vol. 14, No. 3 (1976), p. 470.

3. *Op. cit.*, p. 17.

4. Provisional Military Administrative Council, *Proclamation to Provide for the Public Ownership of Rural Lands* No. 31 of 1975 (Addis Ababa).

5. Refer for instance to Fassil G. Kiros, "Agricultural Land Fragmentation: A Problem of Land Distribution Observed in Some Ethiopian Peasant Associations", *Ethiopian Journal of Development Research*, Vol. 4, No. 2, October 1980; Dessalegn Rahmato, *Agrarian Reform in Ethiopia,* (Scandinavian Institute of African Studies, Uppsala, 1984); Tesfaye Teklu, *Socio-Economic Conditions in Shashemene, Dodota and Dangela,* (Institute of Development Research, Addis Ababa University, 1979); Fassil G. Kiros and Asmerom Kidane, *Socio-Economic Baseline Survey of Welmera Wereda II,* (Ethiopian Science and Technology Commission, Addis Ababa, 1979).

6. Refer to Fassil G. Kiros, "Agricultural Land Fragmentation", *op.cit.*; Dessalegn Rahmato, *Agrarian Reform in Ethiopia, op. cit.*, pp. 47, 55; Michael Stahl, *New Seeds in Old Soil, A Study of the Land Reform Process in Western Wellega, Ethiopia, 1975–76,* Research Report No. 40, (Scandinavian Institute of African Studies, Uppsala, 1977), p. 33.

7. Dessalegn Rahmato, *Agrarian Reform in Ethiopia, op.cit.*, p. 54; Tesfaye Teklu, *Socio-Economic Conditions in Dangela, op. cit.*, pp. 32–34.

8. Alula Abate and Fassil G. Kiros, "Agrarian Reform, Structural Changes and Rural Development in Ethiopia", *op. cit.*, p. 172. ·

9. Ministry of Agriculture, *Annual Report of Cooperative Organization Division,* (in Amharic), (Addis Ababa, June 1988), p.3.

10. *Ibid.*, pp. 5–10.

11. PMAC, *Policy on Agricultural Producers' Cooperatives,* (Addis Ababa, June 1979).

12. This discussion draws from Fassil G. Kiros, "Mobilizing the Peasantry for Rural Development: The Ethiopian Experiment in Progress", in *Proceedings of the Seventh International Conference of Ethiopian Studies, op. cit.*, pp. 577–586.

13. *Ministry of State Farm Development, Its Role, Organization, Present and Future Activities*, (Public Relations Services, Addis Ababa, June 1984), p. 4.

14. Office of the National Committee for Central Planning, *Ten-Year Perspective Plan, 1984/85–1993/94,* (Addis Ababa, Sept. 1984), p. 23.

15. *Ibid.*, Chapter 4.

16. *Evaluation of the Performance of the Ethiopian Economy and Future Directions of Development*, (Report in Amharic) submitted to the 9th Ordinary Plenum of the Central Committee of the Working Party of Ethiopia, (Addis Ababa, October 1988), p. 55.

6

The Outcomes of the Revolutionary Agrarian Policy _____

INTRODUCTION

An attempt is made in this chapter to assess the outcomes of the various policies introduced in the agricultural sector between 1975 and 1991. The assessment is made in the context of the overall socio-economic framework and the strategies pursued by the Government to promote its ideological and political aims and in response to the various problems which it encountered from time to time. Central to this assessment is the basic question with which we have been concerned throughout our discussions in the previous chapters, namely the question of how the policies pursued have affected the conditions of the rural population. We consider first the impact of the 1975 agrarian reform in the peasant as well as the state sectors in agriculture. This will be followed by the assessment of the results of the agricultural production, pricing and marketing, and other policies pursued.

THE IMPACT OF THE 1975 AGRARIAN REFORM

The Peasant Sector

As already emphasized, the agrarian relations of production in Ethiopia were dramatically altered as a result of the 1975 Proclamation on rural lands.[1] However, the pattern of land distribution, and hence of land use, has not changed in any significant way. The Ethiopian rural society today, as in yesteryear, essentially consists of multitudes of subsistence producers, both sedentary and semi-nomadic. The former generally cultivate small and often highly fragmented parcels of land. Indeed, a comparison of the size distribution of agricultural land of the pre- and post-reform periods showed that over 28% of all the producers cultivated parcels of one-half of a hectare or less in 1977/78 as compared with about 25% of the producers in 1974/75 (Table 6.1). This was not, of course, an outcome which could be avoided given the new policy of land distribution among all rural households including those who had no access to land in the reform period. A matter which was of basic concern was the fact that the process of diminution of landholding would tend to accelerate if the practice of land redistribution within the peasant association areas discussed in the last chapter were to be allowed to continue.

It must also be noted that the extent of land fragmentation in the post-reform period was comparable to, and in some places even worse than the situation which prevailed in the pre-reform period. This too was a matter of serious concern, as it might have further worsened unless effectively prevented by government policy. It should perhaps be noted that the cultivation of a few separate plots located at relatively short distances from each other and from the dwelling of a particular producer would not necessarily be inconsistent with the pattern of multiple cultivation of crops which prevails in Ethiopia. It was the tendency toward excessive fragmentation which was of serious concern (Table 6.2).

Table 6.1 Average Size Distribution of Holdings of Peasant Households in 1974/75 and 1977/78

	Percent	
Size (Hectares)	1974/75	1977/78
Under 0.10	1.2	1.9
0.11–0.50	23.6	26.5
0.51–1.00	25.2	22.7
1.01–2.00	25.2	29.3
2.01–5.00	18.7	18.2
5.01–10.00	4.0	1.3
10.01 and above	1.8	0.1
Total	100	100

Source: T. Teka and T. Nichola, *Rural Poverty Alleviation: The Case of Ethiopia*, IDR Research Report, Addis Ababa University, 1983, p. 31.

Table 6.2 Sizes of Fragmented Holdings in a Sample of 295 Households from Eight Peasant Associations in Adaa in 1977–78

Sizes in Hectares	Number of Parcels	Percent of all Parcels
0.01–0.25	382	47.69
0.26–0.38	47	5.87
0.39–0.49	201	25.09
0.50–1.0	128	15.98
1.1–1.5	38	4.75
1.6–2.5	3	0.38
2.6–3.5	1	0.12
3.6+	1	0.12
Total	801	100

Source: "Agricultural Land Fragmentation...." *op. cit.*, p. 5.

The development of producers' cooperatives might have been seen as the ultimate solution to the problem of small landholding and fragmentation. As noted above, the achievement in this area was, however, exceedingly small. It was reported that up to 1987/88, only about 5% of the peasantry had joined agricultural producers' cooperatives most of which were in the stage of *malba*. Moreover, only about 13% of all the cooperatives had yet fulfilled the formal requirement to qualify as *bona fide* cooperatives (Annex 6.1).

The question might be raised as to why progress in this area was so slow in spite of the high priority given to the promotion of producers' cooperatives and the various incentives provided to those who would join. No nation-wide study has been made to find the answer to this question. However, the data available suggest that this might have been in part due to the relatively poor performance of the cooperatives. The crop yields obtained from the cooperative farms were reported to be much lower than those from private peasant holdings and state farms (Table 6.3). It was

Table 6.3 Estimates of Yields of Major Crops in Ethiopia for Producers' Cooperatives, Private Peasant Holdings and State Farms — 1979/80–1985/86

	(Quintals Per Hectare)		
Year	Cooperatives	Private Peasant Holdings	State Farms
1979/80	8.29	12.46	15.66
1980/81	8.15	11.61	13.77
1981/82	6.70	11.20	14.76
1982/83	8.33	12.96	14.78
1983/84	6.04	11.15	14.84
1984/85	6.29	8.23	16.32
1985/86	7.47	8.86	18.02

Source: Wegenie Yirko, "The Development of Agricultural Producers' Cooperatives in Ethiopia: Cases from Arsi Region", *Masters' Thesis*, Department of Economics, Addis Ababa University, (June 1989), p. 78.

similarly noted by one researcher, based on a sample survey, that the producers' cooperatives did not seem to be viable in terms of "average cultivated land, average production, and annual earning."[2] Another study indicated problems relating to "the quality of cooperatives..., peasants' understanding of the problems of collectives, practice of scientific method of recording performance and distribution, participative leadership..."[3]

Quite likely, therefore, many factors accounted for the slow development of agricultural producers' cooperatives. The fundamental explanation was, however, the fact that collectivization in the Ethiopian context amounted to a giant leap from an extremely "individualistic" form of production, to a highly "socialistic" system, with all the economic, political, social, cultural as well as behavioral changes which this would imply. It did not appear that Ethiopia's revolutionaries had paid much attention to Lenin's words of caution in this respect:

> "...such tremendous changes in the lives of tens of millions of people as the transition from small individual peasant farming to collective farming, affecting as they do the most deep-going roots of peasants' way of life and their mores, can only be accomplished by long effort and only when necessity compels people to reshape their lives."[4]

It would seem that the peasant associations and service cooperatives could have played a role as "schools of cooperation". These mass organizations did indeed show promise to facilitate the provision of certain government services and the diffusion of agricultural inputs. On the whole, however, their activities tended to be governed by government and party decisions made at the central level rather than by the initiatives of the rural producers themselves. Moreover, not all the lessons which many of these organizations have taught to their members were positive especially in the spheres of democratic participation and leadership, financial management and accountability.[5] Official reports also indicated that the methods of operation of some peasant associations actually came to interfere with productive activities due, for example, to the many political meetings which they convened often in an untimely manner.[6] It was quite obvious that failure to perform critical productive activities such as ploughing, weeding, and harvesting during the regular periods dictated by natural conditions had serious consequences in the circumstances of subsistence producers.

There was also no doubt that the peasant associations were being used by the Government as instruments of central political control. This could be inferred from some of the official functions assigned to them (Annex 5.1). Indeed, in many cases the leaders of the peasant associations and producers' cooperatives exercised no less powers of control and coercion over the peasantry than the traditional local chiefs of yesteryear. Corruption and abuse of power, moreover, became rampant within many peasant associations and producers' cooperatives. The life styles of many of the leaders of the mass organizations often came to be conspicuously higher than those of the ordinary members whose conditions hardly improved, and more often worsened than before. This is a matter to which we shall return later on in this chapter.

The State Sector in Agriculture

As explained in the last chapter, the Government had placed much emphasis on the creation of new organizations in all economic sectors consistent with its overall policy of "socialization" of the economy. The agricultural sector is unmatched in this respect by other sectors of the economy.

Few studies are available pertaining to the performance of the new organizations. Still, it is not difficult to realize that the creation of new government organizations not only entailed large amounts of expenditure, but also tended to aggravate the problems of coordination of activities. Some of the new ministries which were created in the agricultural sector, for example, could not be justified on such grounds.

Of all the new governmental organizations, the State Farms and the Agricultural Marketing Corporation call for closer examination and evaluation.

The State Farms

The objectives, organizational structure and operations of state farms were subjected to a close scrutiny in 1986 by a special study team which was set up for this purpose. The dissatisfaction with the performance of the state farms was candidly acknowledged by the study team. Major expansion of state farms was undertaken during the economic campaign period which was discussed. As the report of the study team put it, initially state farm "expansion was taken as a panacea for food, raw material and exportable agricultural crops shortage [and was aimed at] increasing production at any cost."[7]

As explained in the last chapter, an organizational hierarchy of corporations, enterprises and farms was created encompassing the activities in different regions of the country. The study found the organizational structure of state farms to be highly bureaucratic and unmanageable.

"For a mere 200,000 hectares of cultivated area, there are several corporations and enterprises. The problem is not only that of additional overhead costs, as such, but also accountability, decision-making, authority at production levels and particularly deployment of skilled staff... Of the total management staff at the farm level, only 19% are graduates while at the enterprise and corporation levels the figures are 47% and 56% respectively."[8]

The objectives pursued and the *modus operandi* of state farms were reflected in their financial performance. It was already shown that state farms absorbed the lion's share of technological inputs available. They were also supplied with a large number of skilled manpower, as well as with the major share of the Government's capital expenditure in the agricultural sector (Table 6.4). Yet, as the report cited above put it, "if

Table 6.4   Actual Capital Expenditure in Agriculture and The Share of State Farms — 1979–1985 (in million Birr)

| | | | | Percentage Share | |
Year	Total Capital Expenditure	State Farms	Coffee and Tea	State Farms	Coffee and Tea
1979	293.3	175.3	–	60	–
1980	507.6	334.0	27.1	66	5
1981	675.7	432.9	53.6	64	8
1982	713.8	424.6	47.7	59	7
1983	731.1	470.7	81.3	64	11
1984	389.6	261.0	26.2	67	7
1985	502.0	334.1	39.2	66	8

Source: *Towards a Strategy for the Development of State Farms, op.cit.*, p. 385.

rentability or profitability is taken into account as an indicator of success, the performance of state farms and related activities could simply be described as a financial disaster."[9] It was found that the total accumulated losses (including those of the Humera State farms) up to 1984/85 had reached 613 million Birr or nearly US$ 300 million at the rate of exchange then prevailing.[10] Out of the total losses, the share of crop husbandry was close to 90%. It might be noted in this relation that wheat and maize accounted for over 60% of total area under state farms in 1984/85 and 1985/86.[11]

Serious weaknesses were also brought to light regarding the application of production technologies by the state farms. Concerning the use of fertilizer and other practices, the following was reported:

"Application of fertilizer by almost all state farms without prior knowledge of soils, crop requirements and the residual effects is a normal practice. The long-term effects of fertilizers being applied has never been given due consideration.

"The necessary data for land evaluation which are the basis for land use planning are absent. As a result, it is impossible to forecast what will happen if present practices remain unchanged, what improvement in management practices, within the present use, are possible, what recurrent inputs are necessary to bring about the desired production and minimize adverse effects, what the benefits are of each form of use, etc."[12]

It must also be noted in this relation that a relatively high degree of mechanized operations, 68% on the average, was applied by the Ethiopian state farms. However, the quality of the technical operations and the level of mechanization in the production of particular crops were questionable. Moreover, most state farms commonly reported about the inefficiencies of the farm machinery, high down-time, frequent breakages, lack of spare parts, inadequate maintenance services, etc.[13]

The economic returns from the types of technologies which were being utilized, especially when applied under the circumstances described, were likely to be much less than optimal. The techniques being applied were, moreover, not sustainable given the total dependence of the country on the importation of the major inputs. The extent of the external dependency increased in proportion to the rise in the quantities and costs of the imported technological inputs and agricultural machinery.

It should be noted in this connection that one of the main objectives of state farms was to earn foreign exchange through exports of agricultural produce. It was found, however, that the foreign-exchange earnings of state farms in the latter part of the 1980s amounted to around 5% of total export earnings and could cover only about 40% of their own import requirements.[14]

Agricultural Marketing Corporation

The Agricultural Marketing Corporation was established by proclamation in 1976. The Corporation was empowered to:
1. purchase agricultural products from within the country;
2. sell agricultural products for domestic consumption;
3. import agricultural products to be processed by flour mills;
4. purchase and sell agricultural inputs;
5. cause to be constructed, equipped, and maintained buildings, silos, storage facilities, etc;
6. maintain a national emergency grain reserve; and
7. promote increased agricultural production through the procurement and distribution of improved inputs.[15]

In the field of grain marketing, its objectives were elaborated as follows:
(a) stabilization of producer and consumer prices for grains;
(b) encouraging grain production through price incentives; and
(c) ensuring an adequate food supply for the public distribution system.[16]

In 1983/84, the functions of procurement and distribution of farm inputs were transferred to the Agricultural Inputs Supply Corporation.

For the purpose of purchasing grain from the producers, Grain Purchasing Task Forces (GPTF) were created in 1977/78.[17] The functions of the GPTF which were composed of the representatives of various government agencies and mass organizations were to facilitate AMC's operations by allocating grain quotas to peasant associations, service cooperatives, and private traders, fixing regional producer and consumer prices, and recommending the licensing of traders by the Domestic Business Activities and Price Control Administration.

In the period of 1977 to 1979, the AMC made its grain purchases through competition with private traders in local markets. However, after 1979/80, grain quotas and prices were set centrally for each crop by region to be implemented by AMC and the GPTF. Grain supply quotas were then allocated by GPTF to subregions and by the latter to service cooperatives, which in turn allocated quotas to the peasant associations. The peasant associations then allocated quotas to their own members. The criteria for quota allocation on the lower levels varied and involved procedures which were not necessarily always rational or equitable.

The policy called for licensed grain wholesalers to supply an increasing share of their annual purchases which by 1980/81 was set at a minimum level of 50 percent, although in some regions, they were required to deliver all of their purchases. Service and producers' cooperatives, and state farms were expected to deliver all of their marketable supplies.

The main preoccupation of AMC was with the purchase and distribution of food grains. By 1985/86, its total purchase amounted to about 56% of the total "marketable surplus" (Table 6.5). The AMC grain sales were destined primarily to the urban population, Government institutions and industries.

The operations of AMC were performed through a network of purchasing, storage and distribution centers. The management and logistics which involved a hierarchy of zones, branches, purchase and grain collection centers posed many difficulties and inefficiences, and necessitated substantial manpower and equipment. This obviously implied much added cost to the Government.

Table 6.5 Purchase Share of AMC in Total "Marketable Surplus" — 1976/77–1985/86 (Millions of Quintals)

Year	Estimated Production of Grains	"Marketable Surplus"	AMC Local Purchase	
			Quantity	Percent
1976/77	50.36	6.54	1.18	18.0
1977/78	45.77	5.95	1.07	18.0
1978/79	47.25	6.14	1.49	24.3
1979/80	74.95	9.74	2.74	28.1
1980/81	63.55	8.52	4.36	51.2
1981/82	62.90	8.17	4.59	56.2
1982/83	77.98	10.13	5.73	56.6
1983/84	63.37	8.23	4.10	49.8
1984/85	42.97	5.58	2.31	41.4
1985/86	60.00	7.80	4.36	55.9

Source: A. Lirenso, *op.cit.*, p. 26.

However, the most serious issue concerning the state marketing and pricing operations had to do with their impact on the peasant sector, more specifically on the welfare of the rural producers and on production incentives. The operations overall were highly exploitative as indicated by the findings of field research.

"First and foremost, quota imposition on grain producers had been increasing without corresponding increases in grain production... About half of the grain delivered for quota in Arsi and Gojam was beyond the marketable surplus derived by subtracting from that amount kept by peasants for consumption, seed, reserve, etc. Our sample survey showed that in 1984/85 three-fourth of the respondents delivered quota grain from their own produce while one-fourth had to purchase grain from local markets solely for the purpose of quota delivery...

"The sample survey showed that grain producers lose income due to fixed quota price... First of all, those peasants purchasing quota grain from local markets incur some losses because they purchase at higher prices but deliver at lower fixed prices... Secondly, the producer prices offered by the AMC have been low in relation to the farm inputs prices that the producers have been paying for fertilizers, improved seeds and pesticides...."[18]

These conditions showed that the marketing and pricing policies resulted in a severe exploitation of the producers and undermined their incentives, a matter which the officials themselves eventually came to acknowledge.[19] Moreover, the network of agricultural marketing resulted in an extremely cumbersome and inefficient bureaucratic system which became a drain on the Government's limited resources, much as the state farms discussed above. The system also opened the door for abuse of bureaucratic responsibility and for corrupt practices especially at the points of interaction with the peasant producers. As a result, the AMC came to be regarded as the single most widely condemned symbol of the new form of exploitation of the post-1975 period.

OVERALL IMPACT OF AGRICULTURAL PRODUCTION POLICIES

The problem of shortages of agricultural produce, primarily food produce, tended to worsen during the period since 1975. The types of responses evoked by this problem were motivated both by its urgency and by the ideological predisposition of the Government. The aim of the Government, much as in the pre-1975 period, appeared to be to raise the marketable "surplus" of agricultural produce as rapidly as possible. As explained in the last chapter, during the economic campaign period emphasis was placed on the diffusion of the familiar yield-increasing inputs such as fertilizer and improved seeds in the peasant sector, as well as on the rapid expansion of state farms which absorbed a disproportionate share of these inputs. The strategy of concentrating production efforts in selected "surplus-producing" *weredas* introduced later on further indicated the determination of the Government to raise agricultural production by more-or-less the same methods.

Within the peasant sector, preference was given in the supply of agricultural inputs to the relatively small category of the peasantry who had formed producers' cooperatives. Any benefits which might have been obtained from the use of these inputs, therefore, accrued mainly to a relatively small proportion of the rural producers.

A basic issue pertaining to production policy concerned the impact of the technology which was being diffused in the agricultural sector in the post-revolution period. Here again the questions which present themselves are much similar to those already raised in the context of the situation of the pre-revolution period. In the first place, the fertilizer and improved seeds technology continued to be applied in much the same way as in the past. The final report on the six campaign years, for example, noted: "Although the inputs are supplied to the peasantry, there is no evidence as to the degree of contribution that they make in increasing production."[20] In spite of the large amounts of these inputs allocated to the state farms the conditions under which they were applied in these farms too left much to be desired. This was already discussed above.

What was the overall impact of the agricultural policies pursued on total production? The first five of the six years of the campaign period (1978/79–1982/83) did result in the recovery of the agricultural sector, though not in the steady increase of production. However, the last year of the campaign (1983/84) coincided with the onset of one of the most severe droughts which the country had ever experienced, resulting in the drastic fall of agricultural production from the preceding year (Table 6.6, Annexes 6.2–6.4).

Table 6.6 National Estimates of Area Under Major Crops and Production of Major Crops — 1979/80–1985/86

Year	Area ('000 Hectares)	Production ('000 Quintals)
1979/80	6056.89	74995.80
1980/81	5678.17	65605.23
1981/82	5652.56	62962.17
1982/83	6087.91	78053.70
1983/84	5732.97	63366.04
1984/85	5864.58	48553.01
1985/86	5985.05	54036.57

Source: "Time Series Data on Area, Production and Yield on Major Crops, 1979/80–1985/86", *Statistical Bulletin* 56, Addis Ababa, 1987, pp. 1–2.

It also happened that the first year of the Ten-Year Perspective Plan was the year of the unprecedented drought and famine of 1984/85. Agricultural production fell by 16.4% during that year which accounted for most of the drastic fall of total GDP of 7% during the same year. However, even by the end of the first half of the plan period, agricultural production as a whole was estimated to have persistently declined at an average rate of 0.4% per annum (Table 6.7). Quite obviously, the poor performance of agriculture during this period cannot be blamed on the problem of drought alone. As official reports acknowledged, numerous

Table 6.7 Estimated Growth of Main Sectors of the Economy — 1984/85–1990/91 (Percent)

Sector	1984/85–1988/89	1990/91
Agriculture	- 0.4	- 1.4
Industry	3.8	- 3.8
Services	3.9	–
Distributive	–	- 0.1
Other	–	16.7

Sources: Data for 1984/85–1988/89 from *Evaluation of the Performance of the Economy and Future Direction of Development, op. cit.*; those for 1990/91 from Office of the National Committee for Central Planning, *Draft Development Plan* of *1990/91*, Vol. 1, p.3.

problems impeded agricultural production, including institutional, technological and other problems discussed above.[21]

THE IMPACT OF OTHER POLICIES AND PRACTICES ON THE RURAL POPULATION

In a society which is basically agrarian, nearly all major national policies are bound to affect the rural population to one degree or another. Here, we outline briefly only those policies and practices which entailed extremely heavy economic burden and distress. Among these were the financial levies imposed on the rural population, the effects of population resettlement and villagization policies, and the Government's passion for bureaucratization and collosal campaign-type operations.

Taxes and Other Levies

The total amounts of agricultural income and land-use taxes collected by the Government rose sharply since 1975/76. The total rural taxes raised in 1988/89, for example, amounted to about five times that which was collected in 1975/76.[22] What is especially important to note is not that the tax burden increased substantially, but that this has occurred during a period when per capita agricultural production was stagnant or deteriorating.[23]

Perhaps more burdensome were the financial contributions which the peasants were forced to make for various purposes. The contributions were collected for such purposes as financing one kind of campaign or another, self-help projects, political activities, etc. The actual amounts of contribution collected are difficult to estimate. However, if the bitter complaints of the rural population can be taken as an indicator, the contributions must have been onerous indeed. Thus, much as the traditional chiefs of the 19th and early 20th century had extracted heavy payment in the form of the produce of the peasantry on numerous pretexts, such extraction was also common in the post-1975 period.

The Population Resettlement and Villagization Policies

As indicated in the last chapter, population resettlement and villagization polices were carried out on massive scales after the mid-1980s. The resettlement policy involved the movement of large numbers of people affected by drought and famine from the Northern part of the country mainly to the South-Western regions. The villagization scheme was introduced manifestly as a strategy for promoting more rational rural habitation, better land use, more efficient social services, etc. In principle, there can be little objection to these polices. It was the lack of any serious planning, and the massive scale and haste with which they were carried out, entailing as they did much hardship to the rural population, which came under widespread criticism.

Considered in broad perspective, the villagization and resettlement policies taken together amounted to collossal attempts to move and relocate virtually the entire rural population in a matter of only a few years at most. The potential economic and social costs of such a feat are not difficult to contemplate. By 1988, close to 750,000 people were found in new settlements most of which were moved in 1984/85, and the villagization scheme had encompassed about one-third of the rural population.[24] Villagization in particular entailed a heavy cost to the rural population, because it necessitated an investment in a new residence — an investment which is ordinarily made only once or twice in a lifetime. This is not to mention the adverse economic and social consequences wrought by the massive dislocations of the rural population.[25] These consequences of the policies of population settlement or villagization have not been documented in full. It is doubtful whether in fact that they can ever be fully assessed.

Bureaucratic Malaise and Campaign-Mania

As indicated above, a number of ministries and other agencies were created with responsibilities in the agricultural sector. The problems of organization and management of the state farms were also considered above. It was also noted that the mass organizations, such as the peasant associations and the political party structures were hierarchically organized on all administrative levels including the basic unit, the district, the sub-region, the region, and the national levels. The various campaigns of the Government also necessitated the creation of additional bureaucratic machineries for their implementation.

The overall picture which emerged was, therefore, one of many parallel hierarchical structures operating under the overall control of single centers of authority at the national level. All decisions of any significance were made at the central level and instructions for implementation communicated down the hierarchical ladder. The system was not only extremely cumbersome, but also tended to stifle initiative and prevent genuine participation especially on the lower levels.

The bureaucratic system, moreover, necessitated the deployment of large numbers of salaried functionaries and obviously also entailed other costs of operation. There was little doubt that the costs of the excessive bureaucratization were in good part directly and indirectly borne by the rural population.

If the monolithic bureaucratic structures were characteristic features of state and mass organizations, the national campaigns were the preferred modes of operation. Many political, economic, as well as military campaigns were proclaimed and carried out since 1975/76 when the well-known Development-Through-Cooperation Campaign (*Zemecha*) was first implemented. Such campaigns could hardly be expected to produce satisfactory results especially in the spheres of economic development and social change. The well-known Ethiopian adage — "fastened while running, undone while running" — might well apply in this case. Indeed, there are reports for example, that large numbers of people resettled during the 1984/85 resettlement campaign have already returned to their original homes.

CONCLUSION

Although the 1975 agrarian reform dramatically altered the relations of production in the agricultural sector, some of the negative features of land distribution which had prevailed in the pre-revolution period continued to characterize the landholding system prevailing in the post-revolution period. The traditional producers nevertheless came under the influence of a radical ideology which had as its basic aim the eventual total transformation of the rural society. While the rural mass organizations which were created served as instruments for the mobilization of the rural producers for various political purposes, they failed to induce effective grassroots participation, or to bring about material changes in the pattern of land distribution and utilization or in the methods of agricultural production.

With regard to production policy, there was little change in the types of technologies which were being diffused in the agricultural sector or in the number of producers making effective use of such technologies. At the same time, much emphasis was placed on the extraction of marketable produce for domestic consumption and for exports even in the face of declining agricultural production.

The economic, social and political consequences of the policies pursued eventually became too severe to be ignored by the Government. In 1988, therefore, the Government candidly acknowledged the severe economic and social problems facing the country. Economic hardships and external dependency, which had characterized the period of modernization came to reach new levels in the period of revolution. In the words of the former President himself:

"It is not difficult to appreciate the impact of the deterioration of production in [agriculture]... the fall in the rate of growth of agricultural production has meant a worsening in the country's food deficit situation... Thus, our *dependence on the rest of the world with regard to food supply has worsened rather than improved.* The negative effect which this dependence has cast on the long history and honor of our country and its people is well recognized... *It is hardly necessary to dwell upon the hardships* which the declining productivity of agriculture has brought on the country and its people during the past five years."[26] (Italics added).

The regime, therefore, declared a new economic policy, the so-called "mixed-economy policy", which it could barely begin to implement as it was fast approaching its demise.

Annexes to Chapter 6

Annex 6.1 Agricultural Producers' Cooperatives Established up to 1987/88 by Region

Region	Stages Malba	Stages Welba	Total	Registered	Number of Members
Arsi	77	326	403	75	39,677
Bale	60	63	123	15	5,704
Eritrea	6	4	10	–	299
Gamo Gofa	16	9	25	9	3,509
Gojam	612	37	649	97	72,131
Gondar	163	5	168	37	12,895
Harerghe	68	222	290	70	27,987
Illubabor	60	1	61	2	2,224
Kefa	109	3	112	3	3,331
Shewa	660	218	878	79	43,812
Sidamo	46	–	46	10	13,799
Tigray	–	3	3	–	174
Wellega	184	62	246	22	11,638
Wello	196	79	275	24	34,418
Total	2,257	1,032	3,289	433	271,598

Source: *Annual Report of Cooperative Organization Division, op.cit.,* p. 42.

Annex 6.2 Estimates of Production of Major Crops for Private Holdings — 1979/80–1983/84 ('000 Quintals)

Types of Crops by Season	1979/80	1983/84
Cereals		
Main season	58,746.48	52,174.85
Belg season*	2,562.20	–
Sub-total	61,308.68	52,174.85
Pulses		
Main season	9,895.47	6,974.94
Belg season	87.92	–
Sub-total	9,983.39	6,974.94
Others		
Main season	831,31	945.69
Belg season	–	–
Sub-total	831.31	945.69
Total	72,123.38	60,095.48
Production Index	100	83.3

*So-called "small-rains" season.

Source:*Time Series Data on Area, Production and Yield, op.cit.*, pp. 13, 15.

Annex 6.3 Estimates of Production of Major Crops for State Farms — 1979/80–1983/84 ('000 Quintals)

Crops	1979/80	1983/84
Cereals	1,622.41	2,006.50
Pulses	12.69	4.64
Others	46.32	16.51
Total	1,681.42	2,027.65
Index	100.0	120.6

Source: *Time Series on Area, Production and Yield, op.cit.* p. 19.

Annex 6.4   Estimates of Production of Major Crops for Cooperatives — 1979/ 80–1983/84 ('000 Quintals)

Crops	1979/80	1983/84
Cereals	1,034.45	1,086.82
Pulses	103.02	133.00
Others	13.53	23.09
Total	1,151.00	1,242.91
Index	100.0	108.0

Source: *Time Series Data on Area, Production Yield, op.cit.*, p. 22.

References and Notes to Chapter 6

1. For an overall assessment of the impact of the agrarian reform, refer to Dessalegn Rahmato, "The Land Question and Reform Policy: Issues and Debate", *Dialogue*, Journal of Addis Ababa University Teachers Association, 3rd Series, Vol. I, No. 1, 3/1992, pp. 43–57.

2. Tegegne Teka, *Rural Institutions in Post-Revolution Ethiopia*, Paper presented to the International Conference on Post-Revolution Ethiopian Society, Oxford Centre for African Studies, Oxford, 1988, p. 32.

3. Habtamu Wondimu, "Some Factors Which Affect Peasant Motivation to Work in the Ethiopian Agricultural Producers' Cooperatives", *Research Report* No. 21, Institute of Development Research, Addis Ababa University, 1983, p. 44.

4. *Lenin On the Socialist Transformation of Agriculture,* (Moscow: Novosti Press Agency Publishing House, 1975), pp. 187–88.

5. Refer for example to Dessalegn Rahmato, *Agrarian Reform in Ethiopia* (Uppsala: Scandinavian Institute of African Studies, 1984), pp. 90–96.

6. Refer for example to Ministry of Agriculture, Office of Agricultural Development for Central Regions, *Plan of Activities for Food Self-Sufficiency 1986/87–1987/88*, p. 14. (Document in Amharic); and *Evaluation of the Performance of the Ethiopian Economy and Future Directions of Development, op. cit.*, p. 71.

7. Refer to Ministry of State Farms Development, *Towards A Strategy for the Development of State Farms in Ethiopia,* Volume 1, Main Report, (Addis Ababa, Sept. 1986), p. 372.

8. *Ibid.*, pp. 432–433.

9. *Ibid.*, pp. 420.

10. *Ibid.*, pp. 386.
11. *Ibid.*
12. *Ibid.*, p. 214.
13. *Ibid.*, pp. 256–257.
14. *Ibid.*, p. 393; the exports consisted mostly of live animals, horticultural and oil crops and processed agricultural products, which are reported to be declining.
15. PMAC. *A Proclamation to Provide for the Establishment of An Agricultural Marketing Corporation,* Proclamation No. 105 of 1976.
16. Fassil G. Kiros and Alemayehu Lirenso, *Analysis of Grain Marketing and Pricing Policies in Ethiopia With Particular Reference to the Staple Teff,* Institute of Development Research, (Addis Ababa, November 1985), p. 12.
17. These discussions draw from Alemaheyu Lirenso, *Grain Marketing and Pricing in Ethiopia,* Institute of Development Research, Report No. 28 (Addis Ababa, April 1987), pp. 58–68.
18. *Ibid.*, pp. 105, 106, 111, 113–114.
19. Refer for example to *The National Food and Nutrition Strategy for Ethiopia, op.cit.,* p. 65.
20. Office of the National Committee for Central Planning (ONCCP), *Implementation of the Six Annual Plans, 1978/79–1983/84* (Addis Ababa, 1985), pp. 3–4. (Translated by the author from the Amharic).
21. Refer for instance to *Evaluation of the Performance of the Ethiopian Economy and Future Directions of Development, op.cit.,* pp. 68–78 and pp. 108–113; and *The National Food and Nutrition Strategy for Ethiopia, Final Draft, Food and Nutrition Task Force,* Office of the National Committee for Central Planning, 1987, p.42.
22. Based on data obtained from the Ministry of Finance; refer also to World Bank, *Ethiopia's Economy in the 1980s and Framework for Accelerated Growth,* March, 1990.

23. Based on data for 1982/83–1986/87, Eshetu Chole concludes that "the agricultural sector is not an important source of tax revenue." This of course does not necessarily mean that the tax burden is any less onerous as far as the tax-payers are concerned. "Agriculture and Surplus Extraction: The Ethiopian Experience", in *Ethiopia, Rural Development Options,* S. Pausewang *et al.* (Eds.), (London: Zed Books, 1990), pp. 90–93.

24. Fassil G. Kiros, "An Assessment of the Economic Consequences of Drought, Crop Failure and Famine in Ethiopia — 1973/74–1985/86," *Ethiopian Journal of Development Research,* Monograph Series No. 1, October 1990, p. 35.

25. Some of the consequences of resettlement and villagization are highlighted by Jason W. Clay, Sandra Steingraber and Peter Niggli, *The Spoils of Famine, Ethiopian Famine Policy and Peasant Agriculture,* (Cambridge: Cultural Survival, Inc.), 1988; Alemayehu Lirenso, "Villagization: Policies and Prospects", in *Ethiopia, Rural Development Options, op. cit.,* pp. 139–142; Alula Pankhurst, "Resettlement: Policy and Practice", *ibid.,* pp. 128–129.

26. Address of President Mengistu Haile-Mariam to the 9th Regular Plenum of the Central Committee of the Workers' Party of Ethiopia, *Addis Zemen,* Nov. 8, 1988. (Translated from the Amharic by the author).

7

The Undercurrents of Demographic and Ecological Changes and their Economic Consequences _____

INTRODUCTION

The interacting processes of human economic activities and the natural environment were considered in Chapter 2. These processes have been at work in Ethiopia for hundreds of years, intensified from time to time by socio-economic and political forces.[1] Because of the subtle nature of the interactions and the inherently slow tempo of change which they induce, their effects were unperceived for too long or until they culminated in the "silent violence" of ecological disaster which we have come to witness.

The complexities of mutually reinforcing socio-economic and ecological processes defy analysis especially in the circumstances of Ethiopia where detailed historical data are lacking. What we shall attempt in this chapter is to highlight some of the main aspects of these processes which have in the past contributed to the deterioration of the economic conditions of the rural producers and which continue to undermine current development efforts. These aspects include rapid population growth, exhaustion of the productive capacity of the land, and the recurrent episodes of drought and famine. A difficult question for which there is unfortunately no conclusive answer at least as far as Ethiopia is concerned, is the question in what specific ways these processes are interconnected. One can only suggest an hypothesis in answer to this basic question.

The hypothesis which is often implicit in discussions concerning the problem of the environment as it pertains to a country such as Ethiopia is that population growth, reinforced by other factors can be a major cause of gradual depletion of the productive capacity of land under conditions where all accessible land is fully under cultivation, where there is manifest failure to improve upon the old methods of cultivation, and opportunities for alternative employment are absent. Under these conditions, population pressure can lead to the disruption of the ecological equilibrium[2] which may have been reached in a particular region, due to deforestation, overgrazing, intensive land cultivation (e.g. decrease in the number and length of fallow periods), and subsequent soil erosion. These processes may in turn lead to the reduction of moisture and to the increase of the vulnerability of the land to the effects of reduced precipitation, resulting in decreasing yields. Where the depletion of land resources is intensified, desert-like conditions are said to set in which can become a cause of the actual reduction of rainfall through the so-called *albedo* effect. Hence, the expression "drought follows the plough."[3] A stage is, therefore, ultimately reached where crop failures frequently occur, famine becomes a constant threat, and unless otherwise averted, a common reality.

The hypothesis has yet to be supported by detailed empirical evidence in the case of Ethiopia. However, one is hardly justified to question its plausibility because of the correlation of recent events and because of whatever information is currently available would suggest. We consider below first the evidence of population growth. This is then followed by a consideration of the available facts on land degradation and its economic effects. Finally, an assessment is made of the consequences of drought, crop failures and famine since 1973/74 which signified the culmination of the *subsistence crisis*.

THE PRESSURE OF POPULATION GROWTH

The period of modernization particularly since the turn of the century has been accompanied by the continuous rise of Ethiopia's population. As will be shown below, the historical growth rates, and hence of the actual impact of population increase, had been underestimated.

Population Growth: 1900–1984

The result of the first Ethiopian census of 1984 estimated the total population of the country for that year at about 42.2 million. The natural increase of the population for the same year was found to be about 2.9% per annum.[4] Both the total population and its growth rate were significantly higher than earlier estimates for that year. The implications of the demographic findings for future development were far-reaching.

It is quite obvious that the population figures disclosed in 1984 did not reflect a sudden jump in the demographic statistics. They rather indicated the fact that the size of the population of Ethiopia and of its annual rate of growth had been underestimated for quite a long period of time in the past. As a result, the actual economic conditions of the country, and more particularly the conditions in the rural areas, must have been much worse than had been assumed.

Estimates of Ethiopia's population had been attempted in the past by various individuals and institutions. Some of these estimates had been described as simply being wild guesses. Others, such as those made by the Italians in the 1930s were said to be deliberate underestimations intended to support the claim that the country was too small to justify self-rule. Of all population estimates, those made by Mesfin Wolde Mariam for 1957 and 1960 probably represented orders of magnitudes relatively closer to the actual population size of the country.[5]

The Ethiopian Central Statistical Office (CSO) has derived reconstructed estimates of the Ethiopian population for the period 1900–1984 based on various sources (Table 7.1). According to these estimates, the total Ethiopian population was probably close to 11.8 million in 1900. The CSO figures show

Table 7.1 Reconstructed Estimates of Ethiopia's Population Sizes and Growth Rates — 1980–1984

Year	Population (Millions, Rounded)	Growth Rate (Percent)
1900	11.8	0.2
1905	11.9	0.4
1910	11.1	0.5
1915	12.4	0.8
1920	12.9	1.0
1925	13.6	1.1
1930	14.4	1.2
1935	15.3	1.3
1940	16.3	1.5
1945	17.5	1.8
1950	19.2	2.0
1955	21.2	2.1
1960	23.6	2.2
1965	26.3	2.3
1970	29.5	2.3
1975	33.1	2.6
1980	37.7	2.8
1984	42.2	2.9

Source: *Population Situation in Ethiopia — 1980–1984*, Central Statistical Office (Addis Ababa, June 1985), p. 23.

that it had taken the population about sixty years to double, reaching 23.6 million in 1960. The total population subsequently increased by about 80% during the period of 24 years between 1960 and 1984.

The reconstructed CSO estimates reveal that the annual rate of growth of the total population had increased from the low level of 0.2% to 1% in the twenty-year period between 1900 and 1920. The rate of increase subsequently doubled during the period of thirty years between 1920 and 1950, but rose by less than 50% between 1950 and 1984.

The point of particular interest is to see how these figures compare with those which were actually used by development planners especially since the late 1950s when Ethiopia initiated central planning. The total population was reported to have grown from 19.4 million to 21 million during the period of the First Five-Year Plan (1957–61). The average annual rate of population growth estimated was probably around 1.6% during this period.[6] According to the reconstructed estimates, however, the total population had already reached 19.2 million in 1950. Furthermore, the rate of growth was estimated at 1.8% as early as 1945 and had reached 2.2% by 1960 (Table 7.1). These figures clearly show that the population of the country had been substantially underestimated by planners during this period.

The population estimates made by the Central Statistical Office for the period covered by the Second Five-Year Plan (1963–1967) also show discrepancy with the reconstructed estimates. According to the earlier CSO estimates, the total population of the country was about 21.9 million in 1963 and 23.7 million in 1967.[7] However, according to the reconstructed estimates the total population had already reached 23.6 million in 1960 and 26.3 million in 1965. The rates of growth of the population were estimated at about 1.7% in 1963 and at about 2.3% in 1967.[8] However, as already indicated above, the rates of growth of population, according to the reconstructed estimates, had reached 1.8% in 1945 and 2.2% in 1960.

It is quite evident that the population figures used during the Third Five-Year Plan period (1968–1973) were also underestimated. The same is also true with the figures employed during the preparation of the Ten-Year Perspective Plan (1984/85–1993/94). The size of the total population in this Plan was assumed to be 34.6 million in 1983/84, 8 million less than the 1984 census result.[9]

It must, of course, not be assumed that the reconstructed estimates of Ethiopia's population exactly reflected the actual situation. However, they do represent the best estimates available and, therefore, confirm that the population of the country had been significantly underestimated in the past. This situation would, therefore, imply that the actual extent of the pressure of population increase on agricultural resources, and consequently its effects on the real economic conditions of the rural population had been underplayed by planners and policy-makers. The implication of this situation must have been serious particularly for some of the highland regions of the country.

Table 7.2, for example, compares the estimated regional population densities of 1978 with those of 1984. The figures are based on the data provided in Annexes 7.1 and 7.2. Table 7.2 shows that relatively large increases had occurred in the regional population densities between the two periods. Certainly, the population of the country had been rising steadily during this period. However, the large magnitude of the increases in population densities cannot be explained by the growth of population alone. The figures clearly suggest that the population densities of most regions, and especially those of Gojam, Kefa, Arsi, Gondar, Eritrea, Wello and others, had been substantially underestimated in 1978.

It appears, however, that the future presents cause for much greater concern than the past when it comes to population growth. For, as will be shown below Ethiopia is likely to be faced with unprecedented population growth during the next several decades, with all the economic and social repercussions which such rapid growth is likely to entail.

Table 7.2 Estimated Population Density by Region — 1978 and 1984

Region	1978 Estimates	1984 Estimates	Percent Change
Arsi	44.1	67.6	53.3
Bale	6.5	7.8	20.0
Gamo Gofa	23.6	31.1	31.8
Gojam	29.9	50.4	68.6
Gondar	26.5	39.6	49.4
Eritrea	19.6	28.6	45.9
Harerghe	11.6	16.3	40.5
Illubabor	15.0	19.0	26.7
Kefa	28.8	46.2	60.4
Shewa	70.8	111.1*	33.9
Sidamo	22.8	32.5	42.5
Tigray	31.1	36.7	18.0
Wellega	27.4	35.5	29.6
Wello	31.3	46.1	47.3
Total	24.0	34.5	43.8

*Includes Addis Ababa.

Source: 1978 Estimates from: *Statistical Abstract 1978*, Central Statistical Office (Addis Ababa), pp. 20–22; 1984 Census Estimates from: *Population Situation in Ethiopia, 1900–1984, op. cit.*, p. 21.

The Growth Potential of Ethiopia's Population

In spite of the famine and war conditions which have prevailed in the country during the period since 1974, the rate of population growth has continued to accelerate.

According to the CSO projections, the total population of the country is estimated to exceed 50 million by 1990. This would mean an increase of close to 17 million or of over 50% since 1974. The economic implications of this magnitude of population increase can readily be appreciated. Given the extremely poor performance of the economy due to various causes, this large increase of population has certainly contributed to the deterioration of the level of living particularly in the rural areas. The strains which population growth have caused on extremely limited social service facilities are also quite evident.

The long-term growth potential of Ethiopia's population poses even more serious prospects. This is evident from the recent population projections undertaken by the Central Statistical Office on the basis of high, medium and low growth scenarios. It is found that by all three scenarios, the total population of the country would reach 58 million by 1995 and would significantly exceed 67 million by the year 2000. And in the year 2035, the final year of the projections, Ethiopia might have a population of over 251 million according to the high

Table 7.3 Population Projections for Ethiopia Under Different Scenarios — 1985–2035 ('000)

Year	Scenarios		
	High	Medium	Low
1985	43,349.9	43,349.9	43,349.9
1990	49,934.5	49,934.5	49,934.5
1995	57,911.9	57,911.9	57,911.9
2000	67,810.3	67,810.3	67,371.1
2005	80,110.6	79,794.4	78.118.5
2010	95,452.4	94.011.6	90,383.5
2015	114,536.1	110,553.7	104,086.8
2020	138,207.1	130,701.6	118,870.2
2025	167,707.8	154.025.6	134,376.5
2030	204,709.7	180,741.1	150,107.2
2035	251,207.5	210,307.4	165,312.5

Source: *Population Projection of Ethiopia: Total and Sectoral (1985–2035),
Population Studies Series* No. 2, Central Statistical Office, (Addis
Ababa June, 1988), p. 30.

growth scenario, or over 210 million and 165 million according to the medium and low scenarios respectively (Table 7.3 and Annex 7.3).

It is of course impossible to say which of these projections will actually materialize. The projections nonetheless suggest orders of magnitude which policy-makers can hardly afford to ignore. For, the demands of overall economic growth, of increases in food production, and of expansion of economic and social services which would be necessitated even by the low growth scenario would be extremely difficult to meet. (Refer for example to Annexes 7.4 and 7.5 which show the projected work force and school-age population respectively). Hence, the need for the early introduction of an appropriate population policy along with the overall long-term development strategy can hardly be overemphasized.

THE EXTENT OF LAND DEGRADATION AND ITS ECONOMIC CONSEQUENCES

The human and animal populations of Ethiopia are highly concentrated in the highland regions of the country. The continued intensive cultivation of these regions during a period of many centuries under conditions of landholding which impeded its rational utilization, exacerbated by the pressure of population growth, inappropriate land use practices, a stagnant productive technology, and other factors has culminated in the present conditions of near ecological disaster. The specific processes which continue to consume the productive capacity of the land include deforestation, overgrazing and soil erosion. A major survey undertaken around the early 1980s concluded that 50% of the highland region, roughly 270,000 km^2 had already totally lost its productive capacity.[10]

The severity of the problem of land degradation is better appreciated by the rate at which it continues to advance. According to a recent report, the current rate of soil loss in the country as a whole is estimated to be extremely high (Table 7.4). It appears in fact that the current rate of soil loss in Ethiopia is one of the highest to be found in sub-Saharan Africa.

Table 7.4. Estimated Soil Losses by Type of Land Cover in Ethiopia

Type of Land Cover	Area (%)	Ton/Ha/ Year	Ton/Year (Million)
Cropland	13.1	42	672
Perennial crops	1.7	8	17
Grazing and browsing land	51.0	5	312
Currently unproductive	3.8	70	325
Currently uncultivable	18.7	5	114
Forests	3.6	1	4
Wood and bushland	8.1	5	49
Total	100.0	12	1,493

Source: Hans Hurni, *Ecological Issues in the Creation of Famines in Ethiopia,* Paper presented to the National Conference on a Disaster Prevention and Preparedness Strategy for Ethiopia, (Addis Ababa, Dec. 5–8, 1988), p. 10.

In economic terms, it is estimated that the annual rate of land degradation results in the reduction of agricultural production by about 2 percent per year.[11] According to the study cited earlier, if the process were allowed to continue unchecked, average crop and livestock incomes in the highland regions could fall by 30% during the period 1985–2010.[12] These rather daring statistical extrapolations must be taken with justifiable reservations even though the experts claim that "care has been taken to avoid overdramatization and exaggeration of the costs of degradation by basing the analysis on conservative assumptions."[13]

It should be stated that some efforts have been made particularly during recent years to stem the process of land degradation. However, these have so far been insufficient to reduce the rate of soil loss.[14] The implication of the continued process of land degradation for the economic conditions of the rural producers can easily be appreciated. Indeed, it is believed by some that Ethiopia is said to be among those countries of sub-Sahara Africa which have exceeded optimal carrying capacity in relation to the size of total population.[15] Future population growth *ceteris paribus* might, therefore, possibly result in the further deterioration of the conditions of the rural population, and indeed of the population at large. Hence, the unabated depletion of the productive capacity of the single most essential resource of rural man, which is the land, constitutes yet another cause of the current crisis of subsistence.

THE ECONOMIC CONSEQUENCES OF RECURRENT DROUGHT AND FAMINE

The phenomenon of drought has occurred in Ethiopia since time immemorial.[16] The occurrence of drought has, however, accelerated and its effects intensified during the present century, and especially since the early 1970s.

It is important to bear in mind that, contrary to popular belief, Ethiopia's land area largely consists of dry sub-humid, semi-arid and arid regions. According to an Ethiopian specialist in this field, these "peripheral" regions, as he calls them, cover about 55% of the total land area and contain 25% of the rural population of Ethiopia. In addition, of the regions adjacent to the "peripheral" zones, Western Gojam, Western and Eastern Gondar, most of Tigray and Wello, and the highlands of Harerghe are also affected by drought every few years.[17] It would appear, therefore, that possibly about two-thirds of the country's land area is drought-prone. As indicated at the outset of this chapter, it is quite likely that human actions over many generations have contributed to this condition.

The period since 1974 can be described as a period of recurrent drought. The economic effects of drought have been extremely severe, although it is difficult to isolate these effects from those of other factors which may very likely have significant impact on production.[18] This is more particularly the case in the agricultural sector which as discussed in Chapter 2 may in any given season be affected by various types of climatic and biotic conditions. Hence, much of the damage attributed to drought may be the result of other causes by which production is continually affected. However, since the period from 1973/74 onwards has generally been characterized by recurrent drought, the annual production data in most cases significantly reflect the impact of this phenomenon.

Impact on Agriculture and Livestock

The regions most affected by drought in the early 1970s were Wello and parts of Northern Shewa, Harerghe and Gamo Gofa.[19] The actual damages to crops which have occurred during this period have not been estimated in reliable statistical terms.[20]

The statistical data which could be obtained for the period 1974/75–1978/79 indicated significant fluctuations in the production of major food crops, undoubtedly due principally to drought conditions which prevailed in one part of the country or another.[21] The production declines which occurred toward the latter part of the 1970s can, however, in some part be attributed to the war condition which prevailed in the country during this period.

In no single year since 1973/74 has the decline of agricultural production been as striking as in 1984/85. During that year, total production fell to about 60% of the 1979/80 estimate and to nearly 70% that of 1983/84. Most of the decline was unmistakably the effect of the unprecedented drought which occurred in almost all parts of the country during that period.

The above estimates indicate the overall impact of drought on crop production. The effect of drought on livestock has also been extremely severe. As we shall see below, livestock losses have further depressed food production, in addition to depriving most pastoralists of their only means of subsistence.

Ethiopia is reputed for the large number of its livestock. It may well be justified to ask how this is possible considering that millions of animals are frequently devastated by drought and other causes. For example, around the period 1973/74, 80% of the cattle, 50% of the sheep, and 30% of the camels and goats were reported as killed by drought in the lowland areas of Wello, Tigray, Eritrea, and Harerghe.[22] Then again, following the 1984/85 drought, the livestock situation in the various parts of the country was reported to be as follows:

"[Wello]: Most of the pastoral population of the Region has lost its animals and has become destitute... Even in the cropping areas only a few animals are left...

"[Tigray]: Tigray has a big pastoral population which entirely depends on livestock herding... The livestock in these areas are almost wiped out... The livestock holding in the cropping areas is no different from the pastoral areas...

[Harerghe]: Most parts of the Region are inhabited by pastoralists... Most of these people have lost all their animals and are destitute ... The croppers have lost many animals...

"[Eritrea]: The recent drought has wiped out almost all livestock in pastoral areas. The livestock in cropping areas were either sold or died...

"[Shewa]: The few pastoral areas of the region are

among those seriously affected by the recent drought and where many livestocks have perished...

"[Sidamo]: It was in the pastoral areas of Borena and Arero *Awrajas* that one of the worst droughts in recent years was experienced, causing the death of over 900,000 animals, about 700,000 of them in Arero..."[23]

As it should readily be recognized, the effects of the loss of livestock on the pastoral population are direct and immediate. As a result, destitution and death by starvation become the lot of hundreds of thousands of people unless rescued by external support. The loss of cattle deprives the agriculturalists of their most vital instruments of production, the plough oxen. This loss aggravates the effect of drought because it reduces the capacity to produce crops in subsequent seasons. In either case, one of the most serious problems which follows a severe drought has, therefore, to do with how to be able to restock the herds. The gravity of this problem can be appreciated from the discussions further below.

Overall Economic Impact

The effects of drought on agricultural production have had repercussions in nearly all other sectors of the economy. The effects on foreign trade are of particular interest as they reveal the extent of dependency of the economy on external economic relations which are inherently unstable.

The quantities of exports of coffee, oil seeds and pulses fell sharply after 1972/73 and then again after 1983/84.[24] The main cause for the declines of exports was most likely to be the recurrent drought. The consequences of drought are also reflected in the pattern of food imports. As could be seen from Annex 7.6, imports of food items were on the decline during the first part of the 1970s in absolute terms and as a percentage of total imports. However, food imports increased almost steadily since 1973, and at an accelerated rate after 1977. As of 1984/85, imports of food and live animals constituted 20% of the value of total imports, rising from the lowest figure of 3.1% obtained for 1975. Again, factors other than drought may in part explain the increases in food imports. It would, however, be difficult to identify any combination of other factors the effects of which would be as significant as that of drought.

The foreign trade squeeze resulting from declining export earnings and rising import bills is demonstrated by the figures in Table 7.5. Thus, during 1984/85, export values had fallen to about 76% of their level in 1979/80, but import values had risen to over 145% during the same period. There can be little doubt that drought and the consequent decreases of exports and increases of food imports explain this condition to a relatively high degree.[25]

During the period betweeen the mid-1960s and the early 1970s, moderate to high increases had occurred in total Gross Domestic Product. A declining trend of GDP set in following this period. Thus, the rate of growth of total GDP declined from the high level of 6.8% in 1964/65 to the low level of 2.7% in 1972/73. By 1977/78 total GDP had begun to decline in absolute terms implying a drastic fall in per capita GDP.[26] As already indicated,

Table 7.5 Percent Changes of Export and Import Values — 1979/80–1984/85 (1979/80 = 100%)

Year	Export Values (%)	Import Values (%)
1979/80	100	100
1980/81	86.7	107.9
1981/82	79.3	119.6
1982/83	82.5	120.8
1983/84	94.7	144.8
1984/85	75.7	145.5

Source: Computed on the basis of data obtained from National Bank of Ethiopia, *Annual Report* 1985/86, Annex 11.

it was following that year that the economic campaign was launched by the Government. Following a period of recovery, total GDP again fell by 3.7% in 1983/84 and by 6.7% in 1984/85. The significant declines reflected the drastic fall in agricultural production mainly due to drought. It is important to recognize that the declines in total GDP in 1983/84 and 1984/85 implied the precipitous fall of per capita GDP by about 6.5% and 9.6% respectively. Quite obviously, the fall of per capita GDP of the rural producers must have been higher than these figures indicate (Annexes 7.7, 7.8).

The Cumulative Effects of Drought

A matter which is not generally recognized is that the effects of a major drought are never restricted to a single season. When droughts occur successively in a particular region, the cumulative effects can be highly pervasive and protracted. This is demonstrated by the Ethiopian experience which followed the 1984/85 drought. For example, the year 1986 was expected to be a year of favorable rainfall in many parts of the country.[27] However, in spite of the relatively favorable rainfall, production was hampered by a number of problems directly attributed to the drought and famine conditions which prevailed during the preceding years. The two most serious of these problems were the lack of seeds and plough oxen.

> "The destitutes in the famine areas were with no seed, oxen and farm implements, and their chance of becoming productive again depended on the assistance they could receive. In spite of the tremendous efforts made, the result was disappointing."[28]

Grain supplies which could be used as seeds were extremely short in the market. The price of whatever supply was found in the market was literally prohibitive. For instance, it was reported that in Wello the price of sorghum during the sowing period ranged between 700 and 1000 Birr per quintal (roughly US

$380–480 at the exchange rate then prevailing).[29] This is equivalent to around four times the estimated annual per capita income of the rural population during a "normal" year!

The extremely heavy losses of the livestock of the country due to drought especially in 1984/85 made it extremely difficult to have access to plough oxen on the part of the cultivators. Little could be done to assist the rural population with the supply of oxen or of seeds.[30]

As a result of these conditions, many of the croppers were forced to let their land lie fallow in spite of the coming of the long-awaited rains. Hence, in Wello, about 20–30% of the usual cropping area could not be planted; in Harerghe, only 30% of the land was planted to sorghum where the usual size of land devoted to this crop was 65%. The increase in production obtained in 1986 was, therefore, much less than potential.

The consequences of droughts to the pastoralists were similarly protracted. The rains in 1986 allowed the grass to appear again in many areas. Alas! There were few animals to benefit from it. Nor were there likely to be many in the short run as it would take time to rebuild the stock of animals, and this only if rainfall conditions would continue to be favorable.

CONCLUSION

The inexorable processes of rapid population growth, severe degradation of agricultural land, drought and famine, therefore, pose enormous development challenges in Ethiopia. These are challenges which cannot be addressed by means of short-term macroeconomic policies alone, but more importantly by means of long-term development planning, resource conservation and the application of appropriate technology.

We have not in this chapter dwelt on the human dimension of natural and man-made disasters in Ethiopia. The effects in terms both of the staggering magnitudes of the population thrown into destitution and often reduced to begging, joining the hordes of those who already crowd the churchyards and streets of cities such as Addis Ababa, and the anguish and ignoble death inflicted on unknown numbers were noted in earlier chapters. What perhaps should be reiterated in conclusion is the fact that the demographic and ecological processes outlined above and their potentially dire consequences are much more a cause of concern for the future than the past.

Annexes to Chapter 7

Annex 7.1 Estimate of Rural and Urban Population — 1978 ('000)

Region	Total	Rural	Urban	Percent Urban
Arsi	1,084.7	992.1	92.6	8.5
Bale	830.0	786.2	43.8	5.3
Gondar	1,942.4	1,799.4	143.0	7.4
Eritrea	2,295.8	1,672.7	623.1	27.1
Gamo Gofa	946.3	905.2	41.1	4.3
Gojam	1,927.6	1,760.2	167.4	8.7
Harerghe	2,955.4	2,715.5	239.9	8.1
Illubabor	764.0	716.5	47.5	6.2
Kefa	1,527.5	1,410.5	117.0	7.7
Shewa	6,055.2	4,474.0	1,581.2	27.1
Sidamo	2,654.9	2,467.3	187.6	7.1
Tigray	2,044.4	1,874.1	170.3	8.4
Wellega	1,910.4	1,806.0	104.1	5.5
Wello	2,469.6	2,309.1	160.5	6.5
Total	29,408.2	25,688.8	3,719.4	12.6

Source: *Statistical Abstract 1978*, Central Statistical Office (Addis Ababa), p. 25.

Annex 7.2 Total Population of Ethiopia by Region, Rural and Urban — 1984 ('000)

Region	Total	Rural	Urban	Percent Urban
Arsi	1,662.2	1,529.1	133.1	8.01
Bale	1,006.5	929.3	72.2	7.67
Gamo Gofa	1,248.0	1,174.8	73.3	5.87
Gojam	3,244.9	2,981.5	263.4	8.12
Gondar	2,905.4	2,681.8	223.6	7.69
Eritrea	2,614.7	2,207.6	407.1	15.57
Harerghe	4,151.7	3,837.1	314.6	7.50
Illubabor	963.3	897.2	66.2	6.87
Kefa	2,450.4	2,299.5	150.8	6.16
Shewa	8,090.6	7.341.3	749.3	9.26
Sidamo	3,790.6	3,541.4	249.2	6.57
Tigray	2,409.7	2,211.6	198.0	8.22
Wellega	2,369.7	2,226.3	143.4	6.05
Wello	3,609.9	3,359.8	250.1	7.03
Asseb Adm.	89.3	58.3	31.0	34.76
Addis Ababa	1,412.6	–	1,412.6	100.0
Total	42,019.5	37,276.6	4,742.9	11.3

Source: *Population and Housing Census Preliminary Report*, Central Statistical Office (Addis Ababa, 1984), p. 15.

Annex 7.3 Projected Crude Rates of Population Growth — 1985–2035

Period	High Variant	Medium Variant	Low Variant
1985–1900	2.87	2.87	2.87
1900–1995	3.01	3.01	3.01
1995–2000	3.20	3.20	3.07
2000–2005	3.39	3.31	3.00
2005–2010	3.57	3.33	2.96
2010–2015	3.71	3.35	2.86
2015–2020	3.83	3.35	2.69
2020–2025	3.94	3.34	2.48
2025–2030	4.07	3.25	2.24
2030–2035	4.18	3.08	1.95

Source: Central Statistical Office, *Population Projection of Ethiopia: Total and Sectoral (1985–2035)*, (Addis Ababa, June 1988), p. 31.

Annex 7.4 Projected Working-Age Population (10 years and above) of Ethiopia According to Different Scenarios of Population Growth — 1985–2035

Projection	Working Age Population ('000) Total	Rate of Growth
High Scenario		
1985	18,709.5	–
1995	24,826.3	2.85
2005	33,718.0	3.06
2015	47,671.4	3.46
2025	69,456.3	3.76
2035	103,257.8	3.97
Medium Scenario		
1985	18,709.5	–
1995	24,826.3	2.83
2005	33,718.1	3.06
2015	47,528.8	3.43
2025	67,562.5	3.52
2035	95,572.6	3.47
Low Scenario		
1985	18,709.5	–
1995	24,826.3	2.83
2005	33,718.1	3.06
2015	46,721.6	3.26
2025	63,852.9	3.12
2035	84,211.4	2.77

Source: *Population Projection of Ethiopia: Total and Sectoral* (*1985–2035*), *op.cit.*, p. 34.

Annex 7.5 Projected School-Age Population According to Three Projections of Total Population — 1985–2035 ('000)

Projection	Year					
	1985	1995	2005	2015	2025	2035
Primary School Age Population (7–12 years)						
High Variant	7,550.8	9,213.1	13,265.2	19,570.7	29,098.9	43,962.5
Medium Variant	7,550.8	9,213.1	13,283.7	18,801.2	25,593.2	34,375.0
Low Variant	7,550.8	9,213.1	13,093.7	16,964.2	20,804.1	23,081.2
Lower Secondary (13–14 years)						
High Variant	1,982,1	2,647.5	3,769.7	5,502.2	8,183.9	12,286.0
Medium Variant	1,982.1	2,647.5	3,766.9	5,446.2	7,468.4	10,196.6
Low Variant	1,982.1	2,647.5	3,784.0	5,069.7	6,413.2	7,445.5
Secondary (15–18 years)						
High Variant	3,226.9	5,400.7	6,837.2	9,702.8	14,426.8	21,622.7
Medium Variant	3,226.9	5,400.7	6,837.2	9,697.4	13,504.5	18,484.0
Low Variant	3,226.9	5,400.7	6,838.3	9,335.5	11,929.1	14,312.0

Source:*Population of Ethiopia: Total and Sectoral (1985–2035), op.cit.,* p. 35.

Annex 7.6 Value of Imports of Food and Live Animals — 1970–1984/85 (Million Birr)

Year	1 Food and Live Animals	2 Total Imports	3 Percent (1/2)
1970	31.5	429.1	7.3
1971	28.6	469.5	6.1
1972	20.0	435.6	4.6
1973	20.6	448.2	4.6
1974	22.3	590.3	3.8
1975	19.8	647.9	3.1
1976	31.6	729.5	4.3
1977	29.7	823.8	3.6
1978	41.5	1071.0	3.9
1979	61.1	1175.1	5.2
1980	92.4	1541.9	6.0
1981	111.9	1528.9	7.3
1982	124.5	1627.9	7.7
1983	214.9	1813.3	11.9
1984/85	345.0	1770.4	20.0

Source: Computed on the basis of data from *Annual Reports,*1972, 1977, 1981, 1983, 1984/85, National Bank of Ethiopia, Addis Ababa; data for 1973 obtained from *Statistical Abstract of Ethiopia,* 1975, Central Statistical Office, Addis Ababa.

Annex 7.7 Gross Domestic Product at Constant Factor Cost of 1960/61 —68/69–1979/80 (in Millions of Birr)

Year	Total GDP	Agricultural GDP	Non-Agricultural GDP
1968/69	3331.1	1791.4	1539.7
1969/70	3451.4	1833.3	1618.1
1970/71	3606.1	1870.3	1735.8
1971/72	3777.8	1936.8	1841.0
1972/73	3879.6	1950.8	1928.8
1973/74	3936.0	1940.1	1995.9
1974/75	3939.5	1902.6	2036.9
1975/76	4031.4	1953.7	2077.7
1976/77	4055.3	1952.8	2102.5
1977/78	4009.3	1922.8	2087.1
1978/79	4221.7	1968.4	2253.3
1979/80	4456.2	2062.2	2394.0

Source: *Annual Reports,* 1977, 1980. National Bank of Ethiopia, Addis Ababa.

Annex 7.8 Gross Domestic Product at Constant 1980/81 Factors Cost — 1980/81–1985/86 (in Millions of Birr)

Year	Total GDP	Agricultural GDP	Non-Agricultural GDP
1980/81	8096.4	4071.5	4024.9
1981/82	8192.9	4019.3	4173.6
1982/83	8629.8	4208.9	4420.9
1983/84	8315.1	3792.5	4522.2
1984/85	7765.5	3177.3	4588.2
1985/86	8641.1	3859.7	4781.4

Source: *Annual Report* 1984/85, National Bank of Ethiopia, Addis Ababa; *Three-Year Development Plan* (*1986/87–1988/89*), Office of the National Committee for Central Planning, Addis Ababa.

References and Notes to Chapter 7

1. Some sections of this chapter draw from Fassil G. Kiros "An Assessment of the Economic Consequences of Drought, Crop Failure and Famine in Ethiopia — 1973/74 – 1985/ 86," Paper presented to the Conference on Environmental Stress and Political Conflicts in Africa, The Royal Swedish Academy of Sciences, Stockholm, December 13–15, 1988.

2. Refer on this point to John J. Hidore, *et al.*, "Climatic Change and Economic Development", *African Environment, Special Report* 1, Paul Richards, (Ed.), (International African Institute, London, 1975), p. 25; refer also to Adrian P. Wood, "Natural Resource Management and Rural Development in Ethiopia", in *Ethiopia, Rural Development Options, op. cit.*, pp. 191–192.

3. Refer to M.H. Glantz, *et al.*, "Cultivating Agricultural Marginal Lands: Drought Follows the Plough", National Centre for Atmospheric Research, June, 1985, p. 4.

4. Central Statistical Office, *Population and Housing Census Preliminary Report,* Addis Ababa, 1984, p. 15.

5. Central Statistical Office, *Population Situation in Ethiopia — 1900–1984,* Addis Ababa, June, 1985.

6. Refer to Imperial Ethiopian Government, *Second Five-Year Development Plan, 1963–1967*, Addis Ababa, 1962, p. 41.

7. Central Statistical Office, *Statistical Abstract 1967 and 1968*, Addis Ababa, p. 23.

8. *Ibid.*

9. Provisional Military Government of Socialist Ethiopia, *Ten-Year Perspective Plan, 1984/85–1993/94*, Addis Ababa, 1984, p. 15.

10. M. Constable, "The Degradation of Resources and an Evaluation of Actions to Combat it", *Ethiopian Highlands*

Reclamation Study, Ministry of Agriculture and Food and Agricultural Organization, (Addis Ababa, Dec. 1984), pp. xiii, xvi, 46.

11. Hans Hurni, "Ecological Issues in the Creation of Famines in Ethiopia", Paper presented to the National Conference on a Disaster Prevention and Preparedness Strategy for Ethiopia, Addis Ababa, Dec. 5–8, 1988, p. 10.
12. M. Constable, *Ibid.*
13. *Ibid.*
14. Hans Hurni, *op.cit.*, p. 11.
15. Economic Commission for Africa and African Development Bank, *Economic Report on Africa*, 1988, p. 63.
16. Workineh Degefu, "Some Aspects of Meteorological Drought in Ethiopia", in *Drought and Hunger in Africa,* Michael H. Glantz, (Ed.), (Cambridge University Press, 1987).
17. Daniel Gamachu, "Peripheral Ethiopia: A Look at the Marginal Zones of the Country", in *Regional Planning and Development in Ethiopia*, P. Treuner, T.K. Mariam and T. Mulat, (Eds.), *op.cit.*, pp. 83–85.
18. For detailed discussion, refer to "An Assessment by the Economic Consequences of Drought, Crop Failures and Famine in Ethiopia — 1973/74–1985/86", *op.cit.*
19. Refer to Relief and Rehabilitation Commission (RRC), *The Wello Drought and Consequent Famine,* Report of the Commission of Inquiry, 1975. (Report in Amharic).
20. *The Statistical Abstract of Ethiopia* for 1975, for example, indicates that there was virtually no difference in the levels of agricultural production of 1972/73 and 1973/74; this obviously could not be taken to imply that production had not declined in the drought-affected regions during this period.

21. Ministry of Agriculture, *Area, Production and Yield of Major Crops for the Whole Country and by Region, 1974/ 75–1978/79*, (Addis Ababa); Central Statistical Office (CSO), Agricultural Sample Survey, 1985/86, (Addis Ababa).
22. RRC, *May Starvation Cease — "Ethiopia Tikdem"*, (Addis Ababa, Sept. 1975), p. 7; other estimates are also mentioned in RRC, *Report of the Commission of Inquiry, op. cit.*, pp. 109–110 and *Relief and Rehabilitation Commission 1973/ 74–1983/84,* (in Amharic), (Addis Ababa), p. 29.
23. RRC, Early Warning and Planning Services, *1986 Food Supply Prospect*, (Addis Ababa, Sept. 1985), pp. 14–34.
24. National Bank of Ethiopia, *Annual Reports,* 1974/75, 1982, 1984/85, (Addis Ababa).
25. Refer also to National Bank of Ethiopia, *Annual Report* 1984/85, Addis Ababa, p. 41.
26. Fassil G. Kiros, "An Assessment of the Economic Consequences of Drought, Crop Failure and Famine in Ethiopia", *op. cit.*
27. RRC, Early Warning and Planning Services, *1987 Food Supply Report*, (Addis Ababa, Sept. 1987), p. 5.
28. *Ibid.*, pp. 5–6.
29. *Ibid.*
30. *Ibid.*

Challenges of the 1990s and the New Century: Conclusions _____

INTRODUCTION

The greatest challenge which confronts Ethiopia in this last decade of the 20th century and beyond is how to reverse the unremitting historical trends of deepening rural poverty and increasing economic dependency. The only response to this major challenge, it will be argued by many, is *development*. Indeed, in a recent report, the World Bank suggested just that: "The primary task of development is to eliminate poverty."[1]

Development, however, continues to be an elusive goal. It is a goal which has been easier proclaimed than understood, and much less realized, as the Ethiopian experience of many decades has shown. Indeed, few issues have preoccupied national and international policy-makers than has the issue of development. Within Africa, nearly all the developing countries have implemented many plans and programs of development. Ethiopia has not been an exception to this. Conditions of poverty continue to prevail not because of the absence of development plans, but in spite of them, and one is justified to argue, often because of them. In this concluding chapter, therefore, an attempt is made to highlight the basic reasons for the general failure of past efforts to overcome poverty. This is based on a critical re-examination of the concept of development in general and of rural development in particular. It is believed that such a re-examination will make it possible to draw attention to the most important policies and strategies required to overcome the economic, social and political forces which have for long acted as the root causes of rural poverty.

THE DILEMMA OF POVERTY AMIDST POTENTIAL PLENTY

Ethiopians were for long accustomed to referring to their country as their "virgin land". More recently, the country has come to be characterized as one whose natural resource base is being severely depleted at least in the Northern regions. As shown in Chapter 7, large parts of those regions have suffered from severe soil erosion. Yet, taken as a whole, the country still retains considerable development potential not only in agriculture but also in a number of other areas. Highlights of the country's resource base are provided in the following paragraphs in order to show that the potential exists for realizing the goals of rural and national development, given the right types of policies and strategies.

The total land area of Ethiopia is 122.3 million hectares of which an estimated 12.6 million hectares or 10.3% is intensively cultivated and 15.3 million hectares or 12.5% is moderately cultivated.[2] (The pattern of distribution of land for various uses is shown in Annex 8.1). The potential arable land is estimated to be considerably larger than the area presently under cultivation especially if some of the marginal lands can be brought to use by the application of appropriate technologies (Annex 8.2). The available agroclimatic data indicate that there are possibilities of rainfed agriculture with one or two growing periods in large parts of the country, and that much larger opportunities exist for agricultural production with the use of at least supplementary irrigation and appropriate conservation practices.

The potential for irrigated agriculture (and hydro-electric power development) can be appreciated from the country's water resources. The country has been described as the "water tower of Northeastern Africa".[3] The annual runoff from the major drainage basins cover vast areas of the country (Annex 8.3). The surface water potential has been estimated as being 111 billion cubic meters per year.[4] To this must be added the potential offered by ground water resources.

Of all the rural resources of Ethiopia, its vast livestock population is probably the most commonly cited. The total size of the country's livestock population was provided in Annex 2.2. The great potential of development in this vital sub-sector is self-evident. However, the productivity of livestock remains to be extremely low.

Indeed, nearly all of Ethiopia's rural resources are grievously underutilized. In spite of the potential of development indicated above, the total cropped area of the country has been virtually stagnant since the 1960s. Less than 5% of the irrigation potential has been realized so far. Less than 1.5% of the hydro-electric generation potential has so far been brought to use. Only about 10% of the potential yield of over 34,000 tons per annum of inland lake fisheries is being currently exploited.[5] This is not to mention the potentials of development offered by other types of resources, such as forestry, wildlife, ground-water resources, minerals and sub-surface energy. It is in the face of such potential that the Ethiopian rural population has continued to suffer the conditions of poverty and chronic famine throughout the modern period of the country's history. In the socio-economic domain, therefore, the dilemma of contemporary Ethiopia can be said to be one of poverty amidst potential plenty. This is a regrettable situation, but it is also a source of hope for the future.

THE CHALLENGE OF DEVELOPMENT IN PERSPECTIVE

Many years ago, a well-known scholar of development studies proposed that three basic questions would need to be asked in order to determine whether *development* was taking place, viz.: What has happened to poverty? What has happened to unemployment? What has happened to inequality?[6] These interrelated questions imply that development is not, as commonly held, only a matter of increasing investments or of raising the total output of goods and services. These are necessary, but not sufficient conditions for overcoming poverty. A matter which is all too often given little emphasis is that development should as much be concerned about the distribution of resources and income among the various segments of society as it is about their allocation to different uses. The question of how equitably they ought to be distributed is obviously not a question that can be answered by economic planners alone on behalf of society. However, planners ought to be able to demonstrate the developmental implications of particular patterns of resource and income distribution. The failure of past development efforts in reducing poverty can be largely attributed to the failure to address the question of distribution satisfactorily. It was generally assumed that as investment and production increased, the benefits would accrue even to the poorest segment of society. This assumption has been disproved by the experience of Ethiopia as by those of nearly all countries of sub-Saharan Africa.

The issue of distribution should be understood in a broad context. It should not be limited to the question of who makes use of economic resources, but should also be concerned with who determines the manner in which they are utilized, and what types of goals and priorities govern their utilization. The review of Ethiopian economic history clearly demonstrates that these considerations point to the root causes of the problem of poverty. The basic predicament of the Ethiopian rural producers has arisen from the fact that they had not only limited control over the basic means of production or over their own produce, but also had little to say about what was being carried out in the name of rural development. As a result, when policies of agricultural modernization were introduced, these actually ultimately led to the eviction of large numbers of tenant producers, that is to say in increasing *unemployment* and destitution. The policy of revolutionary agrarian change initiated after 1974, while claiming to liberate the rural population from age-old exploitation, actually resulted in the *insecurity* of land tenure and in the exproriation of agricultural produce by means of forced grain deliveries or through the more insidious method of "unequal exchange". In the context of Ethiopia, therefore, the alleviation and ultimate eradication of poverty will most fundamentally depend on the resolution of the issues of the control and utilization of basic productive resources and of entitlements to the produce of labor decidedly in favor of the rural producers.

We must hasten to stress that this does not mean that rural producers can be left entirely to their own devices or that they should not be expected to bear their fair share of the costs of financing development or of maintaining the social and political order. They would be better motivated to make the necessary sacrifices for development if they can be assured that the benefits will accrue primarily to themselves. This is obviously not an idea that is new, but it is one which has received little more than lip-service in the past.

The current vogue of development ideology spreading within Africa and elsewhere is that the best interest of rural producers can be served by the adoption of a market-oriented economic system. This would basically mean that decisions concerning resource allocation, investment and income distribution would be governed by market forces with government playing a relatively restricted role. There should be no need to reopen here the classic debate concerning the relative efficacy of the "invisible vs the visible hand". A market-economy policy can stimulate private investment and result in increased output, but it may not necessarily result in the eradication of poverty. Indeed, unless mitigated by appropriate government policy, conditions of poverty may tend to worsen as a result of the *inequalities* likely engendered by market forces especially because of the manner in which such forces generally tend to affect the agricultural sector. We must not lose sight of the fact that one of the most problematic areas of public policy even in the industrialized countries of the West concerns this basic issue which is often resolved by means of agricultural subsidies.

It should be noted that the move toward market-oriented policies in Africa is associated with pressures to adopt the so-called structural adjustment programs (SAPs). The economic and social outcomes of SAPs in Africa are well known.[7] There have been few successes, often because the right compositions of policies are not adopted. If, therefore, Ethiopia succumbs to the pressures to introduce SAP, such a policy should at least incorporate specific measures designed to protect the economic welfare of the rural population as well as that of the low-income urban population. A basic issue in this connection is also the concern of many that the preoccupation with SAP could lead to reduced attention to long-term development. This is a valid concern especially in the circumstances of countries such as Ethiopia where short-term economic adjustments can do little to overcome mass poverty and deep economic hardship which have evolved over a period of many decades.

The foregoing comments have been made with full awareness of the apprehension often expressed regarding past experiences in the field of development planning. Some have taken exception to what they regard as the "blueprint" approach to development.[8] There is also the view that African rural producers in particular are characterized by modes of production and distribution which enable them to elude and render ineffective the dictates of either the plan or the market.[9] These arguments offer food for thought for development planners and policy-makers. It would, however, be wrong to take them as arguments which can invalidate the rationality of planning or the necessity to influence the future course of social change. Even the protagonists of the market-economy policy acknowledge the role that must be played by government in development policy-making and planning. If there have been past failures, these can largely be explained by misconceptions about development or about the role of development planning, by miscalculations, bureaucratic ineptitudes, and human frailties, rather than any inherent fault in the planned approach to national and rural development. It is perhaps essential to emphasize that there is here no case being made for the types of monolithic and comprehensive planning systems which had been characteristic of command economies, systems which permitted little or no flexibility or opportunity for effective popular participation, initiative, and innovation.

It should, moreover, be possible to learn from the past failures and successes of planning. In an important sense, past development efforts could be regarded as experiments, except that too few lessons have been learned from them, and this because there has been little conscious and systematic attempt to do so. Development activities in most African countries have been largely the reflections of periodically changing paradigms and priorities commonly promoted by international aid providers.[10] The rationale for change from one type of strategy to another is never satisfactorily demonstrated, nor the possible outcomes adequately explored. One recent example that comes to mind is the case of a donor organization which had placed emphasis on "institution-building" in one phase of its development aid, but rejected any such aid during the subsequent phase. The reason given was that the funds provided earlier were disproportionately allocated to the expansion of bureaucratic structures at the central government level. A number of questions were raised about the position taken by the donor. Were the expenditures on institution-building at the central level actually unjustified? Were the funds provided to begin with targeted to specific levels of institution-building? How could the institution-building needs of the new phase of development program be met? Could this whole issue be addressed more sensibly by critically examining the past experience, assessing the future needs, setting priorities, and instituting a procedure for resource allocation and monitoring? The only answer which could be obtained was that it was all a matter of policy, as a decision had been reached at the headquarters of the donor organization to draw a development aid program *sans* provision for institution-building.

There was no doubt of course that such a program would be proposed, embellished by the fig-leaves of the current development jargon. The almost predictable outcome would, however, be the regrettable one, that the aid recipient would just as easily make use of the assistance received to suit its own preferences as it would have readily agreed to accommodate the whims of the donor. In any case, the priorities being likely to change during the subsequent round of aid negotiations, the enthusiasm with which the future program would be pursued would likely overshadow the past failures. Moreover, aren't the past failures often the justifications for new priorities? Such indeed might have been the experiences which have inspired the following lines:

It's nice to be the drafter of a well-constructed plan,
For spending lots of money for the betterment of man,
But audits are a threat, for it is neither games nor fun,
To look at plans of yesteryear and ask, 'What have
we done?'
And learning is unpleasant when we have to do it fast,
So it's pleasanter to contemplate the future than the past.[11]

The fault, therefore, is not in planning as such, but in the failure to practise the art seriously and intelligently.

THE SCOPE OF RURAL DEVELOPMENT

The origin of rural development in Africa can be traced at least to the 1960s. The scope, objectives and practices of rural development have varied widely. The accomplishments in general have not been satisfactory however. Partly as a result of this outcome, approaches to rural development have changed from time to time since the 1960s.[12] Many of the activities being carried out in the name of rural development today involve a wide variety of what may be described as "poverty programs" with limited scope and objectives. Such activities have increased greatly in number and variety especially since the 1980s with the rise and proliferation of non-governmental organizations (NGOs). While this shows the degree of interest being given to rural development, it does not necessarily indicate the presence of a planned and coordinated attack on rural poverty.

Rural development ought not to be regarded as a sort of "development in the small" or one designed for the benefit of isolated groups within the rural sector. This would be too narrow and too static a notion of rural development. In order to have any lasting impact on poverty, rural development ought to be understood in a much wider context, founded on a philosophy and principles of development aimed not only at ameliorating poverty but also at stimulating a dynamic process of long-term social change. The need for such a perspective can be better appreciated if the place of the rural sector in general and of agriculture in particular is fully realized in the circumstances of countries such as Ethiopia.

First of all, we need hardly be reminded that the rural sector in countries such as Ethiopia accounts for up to 90% of the total population, a fact which in itself is sufficient to justify the concentration of national development efforts in this sector. For, what is development which does not directly concern itself with the needs of the vast majority of the population!

Secondly, the fact that the rural sector is dominated by agriculture which is not only the mainstay of most of the people but also the primary economic base of future development, should make it of necessity the highest priority sector of investment. In addition to being the primary source of food, and raw-material supplies for industrial use, agriculture in Ethiopia is the source of nearly all of exports and much-needed foreign-exchange earnings, and of a major part of the potential domestic savings required for capital formation. In a country such as Ethiopia, therefore, there can be little hope for overall development without primary emphasis being made on agricultural development.

The third reason for assigning priority to rural development is the fact that the people of the rural areas are generally not only extremely poor, but as already demonstrated they are also prone to become poorer for various reasons including the prevailing unfavorable socio-economic circumstances, inimical government policies, the backwash effects of market forces, or the consequences of demographic and environmental factors. Other sectors of the economy have in the past generally advanced at the expense of the rural sector.

These considerations make it plain that it would be futile to expect that a sustained process of rural development can occur without carefully coordinated actions on various levels. Broadly, rural development would need to be based on the articulation of two types of activities: those, on one hand, geared toward the amelioration of poverty and the rehabilitation of the ravaged rural society, and at progressively attaining the long-term goal of rural transformation; and those on the other hand pertaining to the interactions of rural or agricultural, and *national* development. The activities and measures required for ameliorating poverty would vary depending on the particular circumstances prevailing in particular regions and communities. It will be found in most circumstances that long-term rural development would be virtually impossible without first meeting certain urgent needs required for the very survival of rural communities. As argued elsewhere, this strategy of endeavoring to ameliorate poverty can be understood as an "enabling strategy" of rural development.[13] The approach accepts the fact that rural development is a long-term process, but that the process can be stimulated and sustained by *motivation* from within. Such motivation can result from the initial improvement of the conditions of life. In essence, the "enabling strategy" of development is a strategy which aims to enhance the physical capability of rural people and to stimulate their creative potential so that they are enabled to become themselves the agents of long-term development.

The issue pertaining to long-term interactive processes of rural and national development basically concerns the allocation of investment and resources in general in the most efficient way possible while ensuring that an equitable share of the benefits therefrom will accrue to the rural population. Only under these circumstances should the rural population be expected to bear a share of the costs and sacrifices necessitated for realizing national development goals. In the context of a country such as Ethiopia, the issue becomes one of how to make possible the extraction of potential "surplus" from the rural sector without, as it were, "killing the goose that lays the golden egg". This basic issue must be resolved *rationally* and *equitably*. Development planning at the central and grassroots levels can serve as an instrument for reconciling not only the goals of rural and national development, but also those of meeting the urgent needs of the rural population and the demands of long-term rural change.

LEADING ISSUES OF RURAL DEVELOPMENT

The development problems which face a country such as Ethiopia are many and intractable. In such circumstances, it is possible that basic ills are confused with their symptoms, causes with consequences, and means with ends. The propositions advanced in the following paragraphs have been based on some reflection to avoid such confusions, and to regain perspective of the contours of which may sometimes be blurred by the turbulent tide of socio-economic change.[14]

There will understandably be disagreement about the ranking of the issues of rural development. To some, the politically minded in particular, the main criterion is likely to be consideration of the present and the immediate future. To others, the students of development in particular, it is principally the long-term future.

In the opinion of this author, taking account of these perspectives, the most fundamental issues of rural and national development calling primary attention during the 1990s and well into the 21st century fall in the following areas: (1) the urgent need to overcome hunger and malnutrition; (2) the necessity to enable the rural people to become effectively in control of the means of production and of the fruits of their own labor; (3) the need to devise development strategies appropriate for the diverse conditions of the rural sector; (4) the requirement of appropriate policies and instruments for the better management and utilization of human and physical resources; and (5) the need for the reorientation and strengthening of research for the development of appropriate technology. These issues are elaborated in the following paragraphs.

Food and Development

The question of the relationship between food and development is appropriately discussed in the context of the so-called basic-needs strategy (BNS) of development. A number of international organizations have since the 1970s advocated this strategy. Perceptions regarding BNS have been widely divergent however. The extreme positions taken may be characterized as being "radical" and "reformist". Bibangambah has expressed the difference between the two succinctly as follows: "While the central issue for radical BNS is redistributing power, liberal [reformist] BNS is concerned with coping with poverty."[15] A critical examination of this dichotomy would suggest, however, that "coping with poverty" may not even be possible in any sustainable way without some degree of empowerment of the victims of poverty. Thus, although the problem of hunger can be regarded as a primary focal area of action, it is not necessarily one that can be tackled effectively without at the same time addressing the structural causes of poverty.

While the debate which has been evoked by BNS cannot be taken lightly, the worsening conditions of rural poverty since the 1970s have made it imperative to consider a more pragmatic approach to the problem of poverty. The most immediate issue is not one of transforming society or of meeting all basic human needs at the same time, if at all these are within the realm of possibility in the foreseeable future. The most urgent issue is frequently one of survival in many countries of Africa. Thus, taking their cue from the classical proposition of Maslow, Streeten and Burki have suggested the following:

> "...on any reasonable interpretation, there is not a single level of basic needs but a hierarchy. At the lowest level, basic needs are those that have to be met for bare survival... anyone falling below this level dies (by definition).... At the next level basic needs may be defined as those that have to be met for

continued survival and comprise a minimum of food and water, protection from fatal disease and adequate shelter.... At the third level, the satisfaction of basic needs covers continued productive survival and in addition protection from debilitating diseases, more food and some education. Finally, certain non-material needs may be added like participation in making decisions affecting one's life and work."[16]

In the present circumstances of Ethiopia, and considering the pessimistic scenarios sometimes advanced for the future, it behoves us to pay much more attention to the need of increasing food availability to the rural population in the early stages of the strategy of need satisfaction. While we do not here go into a discussion of the specific approaches required for this purpose, it should be obvious that these would involve a combination of measures paying attention to chronic and transitory conditions of food shortage, temporal and spatial considerations, etc.[17]

It should be obvious that as the problem of widespread hunger and malnutrition is ameliorated, second and third-level basic-needs would increasingly take prominence. The efforts of meeting these higher needs can be facilitated as the people become better able to help themselves once their survival needs have been satisfied. Such an approach is dictated by objective necessity and practical possibility.

It is worth noting, however, that one author has sought to remind us that adequate food availability implies much more than the mere satisfaction of an urgent need.

" ... We [human beings] represent a miraculous transformer of a piece of meat or bread into Beethoven's *Eroica* Symphony, Newton's *Principia*, Michelangelo's *Moses*, a peasant's sown field, or a laborer's length of woolen cloth — in other words, into objects and events of culture in its innumerable manifestations, from the stone of primitive man to modern towns, buildings, libraries, museums, factories and stores and all the complicated infinitely varied aspects of existence." [18]

Means of Empowerment of the Rural People

Successes in overcoming absolute poverty and in bringing about a sustained process of long-term development will depend on what has been described as a strategy of "development from below".[19] This is an approach which places emphasis on popular participation in development.

The term participation is an overused and perhaps abused term. It is a term which like so many others is confused by generic and specific usages. To some people *participation* implies involvement in political activity as opposed to development activity. To most people, however, it indicates involvement in the latter in one way or another. For example, to some people such involvement may simply mean the regular attendance of community meetings. To others, participation means the contribution of labor and/or material resources toward a community undertaking. To others still, it may mean involvement on the part of the people in goal-setting and in decisions regarding specific community projects, or participation in the sense of sharing the benefits of development activities. It is suggested here that all these interpretations can be taken as complementary to each other describing, as they do, aspects of the concept of participation. As the concept of *development* itself, *participation* is also a holistic concept. It is also an idea which like development policy must be creatively applied in particular contexts.[20]

It seems important to stress that the participants in development are not to be likened to something like an acephalous mass with a capacity for spontaneous motion. Development participation does indeed call for organization and leadership, but the principal goal of the latter ought to be to *enable* the people to rise to the task of development.

What are the prospects for the realization of this idea in Ethiopia? In answer to this question it can be said that the situation in Ethiopia today offers promising possibilities for the promotion of development which is based on a wide participation on the part of the people. This is manifested by the institutional foundations which have already been created and by the demonstrated capacity of the people to act in unison for various national causes and for community activities. It is believed that there are very good prospects for increasing participation within the framework, for example, of the peasant associations which have been created. The main attraction of the peasant associations is that they can allow sufficient autonomy to the producers while enabling them to take advantage of possibilities of cooperative endeavors.

In perspective, the participative approach to development proposed here is supported by philosophical, theoretical, empirical and strategic considerations. The philosophical idea is implicit in the proposition that both the ends and the means of development first and foremost concern people. The opportunity on the part of the people to participate fully in matters of vital interest to them is, therefore, basically seen as a concrete expression of a democratic ideal. The theoretical idea on which the proposal is based is that development is fundamentally a creative endeavor which can be stimulated by the participation of the people. The empirical basis is that, socio-economic problems and the development needs and priorities in the various regions and communities being greatly varied, they would call for equally varied responses. The participative approach to development and planning offers a better possibility for the more effective fulfillment of both the community-level needs and the national development goals. The strategic consideration which encourages the adoption of the participative approach to development and planning is that not only will such an approach help redress the uneven distribution of investment and of the benefits of development, but as already stressed, it would also better enable the people to bear some of the costs necessitated by the development effort.

The empowerment of the people by means of their participation in development activities is one side of the picture. The other side concerns the types of national policies which may be adopted in relation to the rural or agricultural sector. Such policies which may include taxation, pricing and marketing of agricultural commodities as well as manufactures, would need to be such as would not result in an undue burden on the rural population. This is a matter which hardly requires further elaboration.

Strategies Required to Suit Diverse Conditions of Production

The economic and social landscape of Ethiopia is extremely variegated. It has been shown that agroecological conditions, systems of production, and socio-economic circumstances vary widely even within relatively restricted geographical areas. These conditions indicate that no single approach of development can be equally relevant in all rural areas.[21] The prevailing problems of production and the potential of future development differ from region to region. Under such circumstances, the overall approach of rural development would have to be one that seeks to respond to the problems and needs in particular regions and communities. This has two important implications. One is that because of the absence of even rudimentary information about the conditions and problems of production, there is clear need to involve the producers themselves in the identification of needs and in the setting of priorities.

The second implication has to do with the agricultural research strategy which needs to be followed in countries such as Ethiopia. Basically, a rural development research system would need to be evolved corresponding to the prevailing agro-ecological and production systems of the country as best as these can be defined at present. This is a subject to which we shall return below.

The special problem posed by nomadic and semi-nomadic people must also be given due attention in Ethiopia. There are those who propose a "rationalization program" for nomadic activity instead of the settlement of the people. This, however, cannot be accepted as a long-term solution to the problem. The nomadic and semi-nomadic populations endure harsh and precarious conditions of existence. This situation alone is sufficient to justify a policy to enable them to lead in time a settled way of life. There is, however, more to it than this. It has been shown that the nomadic people of Ethiopia are in control of a substantial proportion of the large herds for which the country is reputed. This immense potential resource will continue to be poorly utilized, and may even gradually be decimated by persistent natural calamity, unless nomadic herding gives way to settled husbandry.

The settlement of nomadic people, however, calls for careful long-term planning. In the first place, we know very little about the nomadic people of Ethiopia. Many questions need to be answered satisfactorily if settlement is to be carried out with any degree of success. And *success* is important in settlement and resettlement activity, for otherwise future efforts are certain to meet strong resistance.

Utilization of Human and Physical Resources

The most important resources of the rural sector are the people, the land and all the animate and inanimate elements emanating from the land. As already shown, these basic resources are unfortunately significantly underutilized.

The issue of utilization of human resources has more than one dimension. First, it is generally assumed that something around 45% of the potential labor force is either unemployed or underemployed in countries such as Ethiopia. Although the accuracy of this figure may be questioned, it does indicate the likely order of magnitude of unemployment and underemployment that may exist. Secondly, Ethiopia has experienced the dislocation of massive numbers of people since 1974 due to war, famine and other causes. This situation poses a special problem requiring urgent attention on the part of the Government. Thirdly, one of the most unfortunate results of the repressive policies of the Government in the post-1974 period has been the legacy of "brain-drain", a phenomenon which was virtually unheard of before. The actual number of high- and middle-level manpower lost to the country is not known, but it is said to be disturbingly high. Losses of such large magnitudes are deplorable for a country which can ill-afford to lose even a few specialists. Considering all these conditions, it would be justified to suggest a policy of "conservation of human resources" as much as the conservation of natural resources.

Ethiopia urgently requires a national manpower utilization policy integrated with population and education policies. In the context of rural development in particular, such an integrated policy framework is of critical importance in order to reduce the pressure of population growth, and to redress the imbalances in the distribution of educational opportunities as well as in the allocation of high-level manpower.

Policies pertaining to human resource development and utilization cannot be considered in isolation from those concerning the use of physical resources. The development potential offered by the natural resources of the country on one hand, the need for combatting the forces of resource depletion and environmental degradation on the other, suggest that rural development policy in Ethiopia should attach special importance to appropriate ways of resource utilization.

There is here a basic need to reconcile developmental and environmental perspectives. Environmentalist propositions often reflect static notions of resource conservation.[22] Such notions not only reflect a simplistic view but may also at times be counterproductive, and can even lead to absurd outcomes. Let us take an example. In many countries of sub-Saharan Africa, farmers commonly lose much of their potential produce to wild animals which consume or otherwise play havoc to their crops. The wild-life conservation regulations in these countries often prohibit killing or hunting such animals by farmers. Thus, while they can devour and stampede the food crops produced at relatively high cost and extreme drudgery, these destructive animals are not available for the nutrition of the farmers themselves. It must be added that the value of the produce consumed or destroyed by wild animals may be much higher than may appear, as the crops are often produced by the application of such inputs as chemical fertilizer and pesticides imported at high cost using scarce foreign exchange. This is of course not to justify the uncontrolled hunting of wild animals but only to point out the contradictions which can arise when environmentalist policies are pursued without full consideration of their potential consequences.

The key toward an effective "conservation-based" development is the recognition that changes will continue to take place in the natural environment because of either the process of development or the lack of it. In the long-run, therefore, environmentalist interests can be effectively served only if they are pursued in a dynamic rather than a static context.

This dynamic context brings to light a vital pertinent element, one which in fact perhaps more than any other factor sets apart the economically *developed* from the *underdeveloped* world. This is the element of technology — a decisive factor of economic progress which has yet to take firm root in developing Africa. The use of appropriate technology offers the possibility of accelerating economic development without increasing the pressure on the environment, because it makes possible *inter alia* the more rational and efficient use of resources. We need hardly be reminded that in the industrialized world, modern technology has made it possible to produce increasing outputs with the same or declining quantities of inputs of natural resources, and by means of their substitution with synthetics.

The integrated approach to resource conservation and utilization requires certain basic preconditions. The first of these is to introduce analytic methodologies appropriate for incorporating natural resource considerations into the economic calculus of policy-makers and planners.[23] This should permit major investment choices to be made on the basis of the assessment of the costs and benefits of alternative ways of resource utilization. Such choices would necessitate the identification and evaluation of different technological elements or processes. Hence, technology also becomes an integral part of the analysis. The data requirements of such an exercise may appear to be daunting, but this should not necessarily be the case. Even making rough and ready assessments of costs and benefits based on whatever data that could be mustered would be better than making none at all.

The second requirement is to consider technological development as a prime area of investment, because technology constitutes the catalytic element for harmonizing developmental and environmental goals. This is a subject discussed more fully below.

The third requirement for dealing with environmental problems is to introduce a workable planning system. It should be stressed that although environmental, technological and developmental processes are interactive, there is little that is automatic about their interaction. Planning should, therefore, serve as an essential tool for coordinating activities and evaluating outcomes within temporal and spatial contexts.

In all of these respects, little more has been achieved in Ethiopia so far than a recognition of the need for resource conservation in the context of long-term development and some preparatory actions toward establishing basic conditions pertaining to overall strategy. Considering the fundamental importance and urgency of the issues of development and the environment, more rapid progress would need to be made in the coming years beyond the preparatory activities so far initiated.

Research and the Development of Appropriate Technology

There can be no development without a sustained process of technological change. Technological change plays a most decisive role in development because of its influence on all significant aspects of economic and social life.

How can technological change be best promoted in the context of a developing country such as Ethiopia? In answer to this question, as already noted earlier, the first and most fundamental matter which must be firmly grasped is that all technology develops in response to particular socio-economic needs or in order to solve particular socio-economic problems. Hence, in this context, the notion of "technology transfer", for example, is not an entirely satisfactory one since it tends to divert attention away from the fundamental necessity of the indigenous development of technology. This is of course not to imply that technological transfer from the industrialized to the developing countries is always inappropriate or even that the attainment of development goals is possible without the importation and adaptation of some technological knowhow developed elsewhere. It is the matter of basic principle which must be stressed, that is that *home-grown* technology is likely to be the most effective for meeting domestic development goals and for solving development problems.

The need to promote technological change which is indigenously rooted is reinforced by other considerations. Experience has shown that technological change, and indeed development in general, is a slow and long-term process. At the same time, the inability of so many African countries to satisfy even their basic food requirements indicates the urgent need to enhance the productive capabilities especially of the small-scale rural producers which constitute the backbone of the agricultural economies of such countries as Ethiopia. Under these circumstances, greater attention would be justified to the task of improving and building upon the existing methods of production. This is a task which necessitates the better understanding of indigenous production systems, and to this effect the active participation of the producers themselves.

It should be added that rural producers not only can provide much-needed empirical knowledge but can also usefully participate in various phases of the process of technological development thereby ensuring the effectiveness of such development. It is in this way that the people in a very real sense become the agents as well as the beneficiaries of development. Those who may still have lingering doubts about this fundamental proposition would only need to take a closer look at the complex production systems which have been evolved over many centuries by traditional producers in Africa.[24]

It should be obvious that of all aspects of development, it is in the field of technology where the application of human creativity and ingenuity is most required. The role that can be played by research can, therefore, hardly be overemphasized. The wide gap between the industrialized and the developing countries in the field of technology can be explained by the huge investments which continue to be made by the former in this field. Investment in research may still appear to be something of a luxury to many policy-makers facing mounting political and social pressures to deal with the urgent problem of mass poverty. Yet, the basic problem of poverty can hardly be effectively overcome unless increasing shares of the national resources are devoted to research aimed at meeting the immediate and long-term requirements of development.

The need, however, is not for investment alone in the field of research. First, as stressed above, major efforts should be made to make technological change a process of innovation from within. It may be reiterated that where emphasis is placed on technology transfer, it is at the risk of creating dependency of the most harmful type. For, undue technological dependency of nations amounts to a denial to their peoples the benefit of their creative potential and of the opportunity to become the moulders of their own future. Experience also shows that the mere creation of research centers does not guarantee that technological innovation will become a natural social process. This would necessitate the more close integration of research and production, the reform and reorientation of educational systems, and the encouragement and support of innovative endeavors on all levels. The costs of building the capacity for technological development will be high. The benefits are, however, likely to be much higher as can be seen from the benefits being reaped by the technologically advanced countries.

Secondly, as indicated above, in view of the highly diverse agroecological and socio-economic conditions of a country such as Ethiopia, national research systems would need to be "open" systems. This term is used to denote a research approach which does not erect a wall around itself separating it from the rural society within which it functions. The following is an apt description of it:

> "Instead of starting with the knowledge, problems, analysis and priorities of scientists, it starts with the knowledge, problems, analysis and priorities of farm families. Instead of the research station as the main locus of action, it is now the farm. Instead of the scientist as the central experimenter, it is now the farmer... and other members of the farm family."[25]

Thirdly, there is need to give more attention to interdisciplinary research involving both natural and social scientists. Social scientists in Africa play a very minor role especially in research relating to the development of appropriate agricultural technology. One finds, for example, very few social scientists participating in national agricultural research systems such as the Institute of Agricultural Research in Ethiopia, or within the Consultative Group on International Agricultural Research (CGIAR) system. The International Centre of Insect Physiology and Ecology (ICIPE) is a notable exception in this respect.

It should be stressed that social scientists ought to play a much greater role in research pertaining to the development of appropriate technology. For, many of the features attributed to appropriate technology are socio-economic in nature.[26] There is, therefore, much need for social scientists to work collaboratively in an interdisciplinary research framework with natural scientists and engineers, and, of course, among themselves. This is admittedly not easy to achieve. Yet, it is an approach dictated by the quest for appropriate solutions to real social problems.

CONCLUDING REMARKS

In closing this final chapter, a few general comments are in order. First, it should be reiterated that the development issues outlined above are not exhaustive. Second, it is not to be inferred that they can be meaningfully addressed in isolation, as they are closely interdependent. Thirdly, the focal areas of development policy and action will *ipso facto* change over time as development goals are progressively attained and as new problems inevitably present themselves. These considerations reflect the arduous and intractable nature of the development process. It would be wrong to assume that the many dimensions of this process can be tackled by the planners alone. There is a fundamental need for a vision of development by which priorities, policies and decisions can be unified, contradictions resolved, and conflicting interests equitably adjusted. It should be realized that the throes of contradictions, conflicts, and imbalances may be severe in the early stages of the development process. Streeten, for example, reminds us of the early formulation by Pigou of the theory of the Second Best:

"A man ordered to walk a tight rope carrying a bag in one hand would be better off if he were allowed to carry a second bag in the other hand, though of course if he started bagless to add a bag would handicap him."[27]

The quest for a vision of development is compelling in this particular phase of development of the countries of sub-Saharan Africa. With the debates concerning the grand ideological alternatives relegated to the side-line, a void has been left in the development discourse. To endeavor to fill this void is the unique historical challenge of African intellectuals, and especially of the social scientists.[28] This is not a call for a vain research for dogma, but one to rekindle the spirit of rising aspirations which is in danger of extinction, to keep alive the idea that the end of development is man himself, to distill experience, and to rediscover Africa's humanistic tradition thereby to cultivate a harmonious process of socio-economic change.

Finally, in opening this chapter we made the statement that the greatest challenge facing Ethiopia has to do with how to reverse the unremitting trend of deepening rural poverty. The validity of this statement can hardly be contested. It assumes, however, that there will be a definite break with the past in two major respects. First, in the political realm, there is need for a break with mindless obsession with power, with the pathological bent toward regressive authoritarianism and repression, with naked opportunism, and with the shameless pursuits of narrow sectarian interests as opposed to those of all the citizens. These are harsh words, but they have to be said, not merely to lament bitter experience, but more as a challenge to all those who can make a difference to the lives of the forlorn majority of the population.

Second, there is the fundamental necessity for a break with the habit of "excessive mimicry" in all fields[29] and with the malaise of chronic external dependency. Let it be reiterated that this is not a call for autarky. Perhaps it is necessary to restate the basic issue once again in terms of its most dramatic manifestations. With 85% or more of the total work-force occupied in food production, the very survival of an increasing proportion of the population of the country is dependent on food aid. On top of this, Ethiopia has become one of the most indebted of the 42 countries currently listed as being least developed. The country's debt-service ratio (payments to export earnings) reached 40% in 1989.[30] There are those who argue that this situation can be altered by means of yet additional amounts of external donations and financial credit. There is, however, little justification in placing much hope on this prospect. First, it stands in total contradiction to the historical experience.[31] Second, as the representatives of the North themselves are wont to reminding us, there is already "donor fatigue" abroad. Thirdly, the credit-worthiness of a country so deeply mired in debt is not something on which to bank as far as future credit is concerned. There can, therefore, be no substitute for a national resolve to adopt a development strategy which is fundamentally endogenously driven, assisted, to be sure, by external aid, but not dominated by or subservient to it.

Annexes to Chapter 8

Annex 8.1 Ethiopia — Distribution of Land by Various Uses

Use	Area in hectares	Percent of Total Area of the Country
Intensively cultivated land	12,596,900	10.3
Moderately cultivated land	15,287,500	12.5
Afro-alpine and sub-afro-alpine vegetation	244,600	0.2
High forest	5,381,200	4.4
Woodland	3,057,500	2.5
Riparian woodland and shrubland	733,800	0.6
Bushland and shrubland	26,172,200	21.4
Grassland	37,301,500	30.5
Waterbodies	611,500	0.5
Others	20,913,300	17.1
Total	122,300,000	100.0

Source: Ethiopia: National Report, *Environment and Development,* Submitted to the UN Conference on Environment and Development, Rio de Janeiro, June 1–12, 1992, p. 58.

Annex 8.2 Ethiopia — Agricultural Land Use Classes

Land Use Class	Descriptions	Area (Million Hectares)	Percent of Total
Arable Land	– Dependable growing period (DGP) more than 90 days – Soils more than 250 mm deep – Surface stoniness less than 50% stone cover – Vertisols not included – Slopes over 30% not included	34	27
Other Arable Land: Vertisols	– All areas predominantly covered by heavy black clay soils	7	6
Other Arable Land: Steep Land	– All land over 30% slope – All other factors as for arable land	6	5
Marginal Land	– Land with significant moisture limitations (less than 90 days of DGP but more than 60 days on average) – All other factors as for arable land	16	13
Non-Arable Land	– Land with severe moisture limitations (less than 60 days DGP on average) – Soils less than 250 mm deep – Surface stoniness greater than 50%	61	49
Total		124	100

Source: Quoted from Master Land Use Plan, MOA/UNDP/FAO, 1988, by National Report, *Environment and Development, op. cit.*, p. 59.

Annex 8.3 Annual Runoff from Major Drainage Basins in Ethiopia

Basin	Countries Sharing (if any)	Area in km²	Annual Runoff x10⁹/m³
Wabi Shebelle	Somalia	202,697	3.16
Abay (Blue Nile)	Sudan, Egypt	201,346	52.60
Genale-Dawa-Weyib	Somalia, Kenya	171,042	5.88
Awash		112,697	4.60
Tekezze-Angereb-Goany	Sudan, Egypt	90,001	7.63
Omo-Ghibe		78,213	17.96
Baro-Akobo	Sudan, Egypt	74,102	11.89
Danakil		74,002	0.86
Rift Valley Lakes		52,739	5.64
Red Sea		43,692	0.22
Barka-Anseba	Sudan	41,698	0.36
Mereb-Gash	Sudan	23,932	0.88
Total		1,166,161	111.68

Source: Ethiopia National Report, *Environment and Development, op. cit.*, p. 66.

References and Notes to Chapter 8

1. World Bank, *World Development Report 1992*, (New York: Oxford University Press, 1992), p. 29.
2. Ethiopia: National Report, *Environment and Development, A Report Prepared for the UN Conference on Environment*, Rio de Janeiro, June 1–12, 1992, p. 58.
3. *Ibid.*, p. 65.
4. *Ibid.*, p. 5.
5. *Ibid.*, pp. 68, 4.
6. D. Seers, "Challenges to Development Theories and Strategies", *International Development*, 1970.
7. Refer for example to: Economic Commission for Africa, *African Alternative Framework to Structural Adjustment Programmes for Socio-Economic Recovery and Transformation*, (Addis Ababa, 1990); *Adjustment with a Human Face*, Vol. I, G. A. Cornia, R. Jolly and F. Stewart, (Eds.), (Oxford: Clarendon Press, 1987); Thandika Mkandawire, "30 Years of African Independence: The Economic Experience", in *30 Years of Independence in Africa: The Lost Decades?* P. Anyang' Nyong'o, (Ed.), African Association of Political Science, 1992, pp. 98–99; Fassil G. Kiros, "Currency Devaluation in Africa: Framework of Analysis and Experience", *Eastern Africa Social Science Research Review*, Vol. V, No. 2, 1989; A.A. Ali, "Structural Adjustment Programmes and Poverty Creation in Africa: Evidence from Sudan", *Eastern Africa Social Science Research Review*, Vol. VIII, No. 1, Jan. 1992.
8. D.C. Corten, "Community Organization and Rural Development: A Learning Process Approach", *Public Administration Review*, Vol. 40, No. 5, Sept.–Oct., 1980.
9. Goran Hyden, *Beyond Ujamaa in Tanzania, Underdevelopment and Uncaptured Peasantry, op. cit.*

10. M. Feldsieper, "Development Theory, Development Policy and Policy Dialogue. Some Remarks on the Consequences of Thirty Years of Policy Trial and Error(s)", *Economics*, A Biannual Collection of Recent German Contributions to the Field of Economic Science, Vol. 43, pp. 28–39; also Goran Hyden, "Ideology and the Social Sciences: The African Experience", *Eastern Africa Social Science Research Review*, Vol. V, No. 1, Jan. 1989, pp. 50–65.
11. Attributed to Kenneth E. Boulding.
12. Goran Hyden, "Ideology and the Social Sciences: The African Experience", *op. cit.*
13. These comments draw from Fassil G. Kiros, "Leading Issues of Rural Transformation in Ethiopia", *Proceedings of the Eighth International Conference of Ethiopian Studies,* Vol. 1, Addis Ababa University, 1980.
14. "Leading Issues of Rural Transformation in Ethiopia", *op.cit.*
15. Jossy R. Bibangambah, "Approaches to the Problem of Rural Poverty in Africa", in *Challenging Rural Poverty*, Fassil G. Kiros, (Ed.), 1985, p. 53. Various interpretations of BNS are also discussed in Bjorn Hettne, *Development Theory and the Three Worlds*, *op. cit.*, pp. 167–172.
16. Quoted by Bibangambah, *op. cit.*, pp. 53–54.
17. Refer for example to Deryke Belshaw, "Food Strategy Formulation and Development Planning in Ethiopia", *Food Security in Developing Countries,* Simon Maxwell, (Ed.), *IDS Bulletin*, Vol. 21, No. 3, July, 1990, p. 36.
18. Pitrim P. Sorokin, *Hunger as a Factor in Human Affairs*, (Translated by E. P. Sorokin, Edited by T. L. Smith), (Gainesville: The University Presses of Florida), 1975, p. 3.
19. Refer for example to *Development from Above or Below?* W.B. Stohr and F. Taylor, (Eds.), 1981.
20. These comments draw from Fassil G. Kiros, "The Case of a Participative Approach to Regional Development Planning

in Ethiopia", *Regional Planning and Development in Ethiopia* 2, P. Treuner, T. K. Mariam, T. Mulat, (Eds.), Institute of Development Research, Addis Ababa University and Stuttgart University, 1988.

21. "Leading Issues of Rural Transformation in Ethiopia", *op. cit.*

22. These comments draw from Fassil G. Kiros, "Coming to Terms with the Issues of Development and the Environment", *Whydah*, African Academy of Sciences, Vol. 3, No. 1, Sept. 1992.

23. Refer for example to World Bank, "Environment Management and Economic Development, G. Schramm and J.J. Warford, (Eds.), (Baltimore: The John Hopkins University Press, 1989); *Environmental Accounting for Sustainable Development*, Yusuf J. Ahmad *et al.*, (Eds.), (Washington D.C: The World Bank, 1990).

24. Refer for example to *Science for Development in Africa*, T.R. Odhiambo and T.T. Isoun, (Eds.), (Nairobi: ICIPE Science Press and Academy Science Publishers, 1989), pp. 115–129.

25. R. Chambers, *et al.*, (Eds.), *Farmer First*, (London: Intermediate Technology Publications, 1989), p. xix.

26. Fassil G. Kiros, "The Role of the Social Sciences in the Development of Appropriate Technology for the Small Scale Rural Producers", *Dialogue*, 2–11/91, Social Science Interface Research Unit, ICIPE, 1991.

27. Quoted by Paul Streeten in "Development Dichotomies", *World Development*, Vol. 11, No. 10, 1983, p. 886.

28. Although the Social Sciences do not have a long history in Africa, recent advances are notable. Considerable works of social scientists have been published by CODESRIA in Senegal and OSSREA (Organization for Social Science Research in Eastern Africa) in Ethiopia. CODESRIA publishes *Africa Development* and OSSREA the *Eastern*

Africa Social Science Research Review regularly. On the role and methodologies of the Social Sciences the following are useful sources: Thandika Mkandawire, "Problems and Prospects of the Social Sciences in Africa and a Vision for the 1990s"; K. Prah, "In Search of a Tradition for Social Science Research in Africa and a Vision for the 1990s; Goran Hyden, "Ideology and the Social Sciences: The African Experience"; all in *Eastern Africa Social Science Research Review*, Vol. V, No. 1, Jan. 1989. Also *Research Methods in the Social Sciences, A Quest for Relevant Approaches for Africa*, B.O.M. Fadlalla and Fassil G. Kiros, (Eds.), (Published for OSSREA by Khartoum University Press, 1986). Refer also to Fassil G. Kiros, "On the Predicament of the Social Scientist and his Enterprise", and P. Anyang' Nyong'o, "Social Science Research and the Problem of Values", both in *Eastern Africa Social Science Research Review*, Vol. 1, No. 1, January 1985.

29. Economic Commission for Africa, Symposium on the Future Development Prospects in Africa Towards the year 2000, E/CN. 14/698/Add.2, Monrovia, 1979, p.3.

30. UNCTAD, *The Least Developed Countries*, 1991 Report (New York: UN Publications, 1992), pp. A. 50–57, A. 52–53.

31. Thandika Mkandawire, "30 Years of African Independence: The Economic Experience" *op. cit.*, pp. 99–100; Fassil G. Kiros, "What is in a New International Economic Order for the Least Developed Countries of Africa?", *Africa Development*, CODESRIA, Vol. 6, No. 4, 1981; *Indigenization of African Economies*, Adebayo Adedeji, (Ed.), (London: Hutchinson & Co. Publishers Ltd.), 1981.

Index